PRAISE FOR *ASSUME NOTHING*

"This courageous and terrifying book charts the author's descent into an abusive relationship and also her emergence from it in taut, seductive prose. Selvaratnam explains how—even as an educated, sophisticated, liberal feminist—she was enthralled by her lover's fame and tolerated escalating personal violence. Her narrative is vivid and bracingly frank, a tour de force of self-revelation and, ultimately, of redemption."

—Andrew Solomon, National Book Award–winning
author of *Far from the Tree* and *The Noonday Demon*

"In *Assume Nothing*, Selvaratnam very bravely and compellingly uses her personal experience to shine a light on the global crisis of violence against women. An important book for the women's rights movement, *Assume Nothing* demonstrates that violence against women exists across race, class, economic status, and education levels and may be perpetrated by those we think of as allies! It dispels the myth that there are certain types of victims and perpetrators. It will help a lot of people, and particularly those who hesitate to identify as a victim/survivor for fear of losing their grounding both publicly and privately."

—Yasmeen Hassan, Global Executive
Director, Equality Now

"Every woman who tells the story of her own experience of sexual violence is brave. But it takes a particularly strong breed of courage to tell the story of how an outspoken advocate for women's issues becomes embroiled in an abusive relationship, and that is Tanya Selvaratnam's story. *Assume Nothing* is a vivid accounting of her experience, and it demolishes dozens of old clichés in one fell swoop: the stereotype of the typical victim, for one, and the image of the typical abuser, for another. Read it. It has the power to change how we all think—and what we put up with."

—Cindi Leive, journalist; senior fellow, USC Annenberg
School for Communication and Journalism

"Assume Nothing is a gut-wrenching, personal tale told by one of the bravest women of the #MeToo era. Tanya Selvaratnam spares no one, including herself, as she shines much-needed light on the often misunderstood subject of intimate violence. By confronting her abuser, she finds her voice and power to be even greater than his."

—Jane Mayer, author of *Dark Money* and
staff writer for the *New Yorker*

"*Assume Nothing* is a searing account of Tanya Selvaratnam's relationship with one of the most powerful men in New York. In lucid prose, she recounts the confusion of signals—the loving embrace turned choke hold—and her struggle to reclaim her voice and power. This book is a necessary and important addition to the conversation around #MeToo—and a gift to women everywhere."

—Danzy Senna, author of *Caucasia* and *New People*

"Crystal prose, precise and calm, grants Selvaratnam's narrative of manipulative abuse, a profound ethical clarity. A grave book, a powerful and essential book."

—Kiran Desai, Man Booker Prize–winning
author of *The Inheritance of Loss*

"*Assume Nothing* is a harrowing story of the illusions we live with about power and authority and the splits between our public and private selves. This book illustrates how vulnerable we all are; even those who outwardly seem so strong have ancient fractures, points of entry where we are susceptible to the debilitating darkness of others."

—A. M. Homes, author of *The Mistress's Daughter* and *May We Be Forgiven*

"Assume Nothing is a searing, brilliant, and courageous book. Tanya Selvaratnam not only opens the door to what happened to her with honesty and insight but provides incredible resources for anyone on how to get out of a similar situation. This book will empower many."

—Tiffany Shlain, award-winning author, Emmy-nominated filmmaker, founder of the Webby Awards

"No one wants to believe they are the kind of person who would fall for an abuser. But the reality is that there is no one kind of person who can end up in a relationship where someone inflicts partner violence and/or psychological abuse. The range of women targeted includes those with their own significant power, like author Tanya Selvaratnam. Her book reinforces knowledge our society so often conceals, that partner violence is part of the fabric of our society at all levels. Selvaratnam does a delicate job of dealing with emotions and personal histories, including her own and those of the man who abused her, while making clear this is never acceptable, never excusable, and no one should be beyond justice."

—Farai Chideya, author of *The Episodic Career* and *The Color of Our Future*

"Tanya Selvaratnam's *Assume Nothing* is a vivid, compelling, and heartrending story about her personal encounter with domestic violence. It reads like a horror story. 'No, no!' we cry. 'Not him. Don't let it be true.' But it is. Selvaratnam takes us through her own gradual awakening without sugarcoating anything. This is a brave and winning work that will be of enormous help to many people."

—Mark Epstein, MD, author of *The Trauma of Everyday Life* and *Advice Not Given: A Guide to Getting over Yourself*

"Assume Nothing demonstrates how the promises and threats of our patriarchal society corrode not just the lives of its victims but the

consciences of perpetrators as well. . . . Her capacity to see violent men as vulnerable to the claims and rituals of contemporary patriarchy—with its central tenet that tyrannizing others is the goal of life—can be a lifeline to other victims of domestic abuse."

—Virginia Heffernan, *Los Angeles Times*

ASSUME NOTHING

ALSO BY TANYA SELVARATNAM

*The Big Lie: Motherhood, Feminism, and
the Reality of the Biological Clock*

ASSUME
NOTHING

A STORY OF
INTIMATE VIOLENCE

TANYA
SELVARATNAM

HARPER

An Imprint of HarperCollins*Publishers*

HarperCollins books may be purchased for educational, business, or sales promotional use. For information, please email the Special Markets Department at SPsales@harpercollins.com.

FIRST EDITION

Library of Congress Cataloging-in-Publication Data has been applied for.

ISBN 978-0-06-305990-0

21 22 23 24 25   LSC   10 9 8 7 6 5 4 3 2 1

For everyone who shared their stories of intimate violence and compelled me to write this book

To withhold words is power. But to share our words with others, openly and honestly, is also power.

—Terry Tempest Williams,
When Women Were Birds

CONTENTS

INTRODUCTION

Early in our relationship, Eric Schneiderman told me that he could tap my phone and have me followed. Because he was the attorney general of New York State, I knew he had the power to do it. His power was a thread that ran throughout our relationship. Over the course of about a year, I had been broken down by the slapping, spitting, and choking that he had inflicted on me during sex, never with my consent, and by his gaslighting, which had destroyed my self-esteem.

"Don't be afraid. Don't be ashamed," I told myself every day in the months before my story of abuse became public. I had decided to come forward after I had realized I was part of a pattern. It wasn't just my story; other women shared it. And I had to tell it to help prevent still others from having it become their story, too.

In early January 2018, I spoke with David Remnick, the editor of the *New Yorker*, about my experience with Eric. I gave Remnick my word that I wouldn't talk to other publications while he decided how to proceed. He told me that if I were alone in coming forward, I could be in peril.

On March 20, my birthday, *New Yorker* staff writer Jane Mayer called me at Remnick's request, wanting to hear about my experience in my own words. After hearing me describe it in great detail, she echoed Remnick's opinion: if I were alone in coming forward, I could be in peril. She asked me to give her time while she tried to contact previous girlfriends of Eric. Within two weeks, she had spoken with two of them, and their stories were eerily similar to mine.

At that point, I knew that the story's coming out was inevitable. I also knew that despite being terrified, I had to participate on the record to give it weight. Moreover, I knew deep down that I was doing the right thing, and I had clear objectives: to warn other women about him and to highlight the hypocrisy of men who claim to be champions of women publicly but abuse them privately.

Eric would often say "Assume nothing." He would also say "Trust no one." In my relationship with Eric, I went through the classic stages that structure intimate partner violence, stages that many victims go through: entrapment, isolation, control, demeaning, and abuse. My story is a testament to what survivors of intimate partner violence experience, and how long it can take to recognize and name the abuse.

In speaking out, I was determined to present my own behavior, as humiliating as the details were. I was making myself vulnerable in a way I didn't want to. It would have been far easier to move on and do nothing; I would much rather have gone on with my life and not gotten caught up in the mess of coming forward. But if ever there was a moment to come forward, I saw, this was the time, against the backdrop of Me Too and Time's Up.

After the *New Yorker* article came out, I worked hard to understand how I had gotten into a relationship with a man who had made me feel so bad about myself. I had a long bridge to cross before I could be in an intimate relationship again. As a child, I had witnessed domestic violence in my home, my father beating my mother. I had never thought I would become a victim. A friend said he had been shocked about what had happened to me because he thought of me as fierce, independent, and an advocate for women's rights and safety. But when I met Eric, I was on a trajectory of recovering from a series of health issues (multiple miscarriages and cancer) followed by a divorce. I was secure with regard to my work and my friendships, but I was weakened with regard to romance. Then my path intersected with that of Eric, who I would later discover had a history of breaking strong women down. I was ripe for the breaking. It was the perfect storm.

I want to shift the perception of what a victim looks like. A victim looks like all of us. According to the National Coalition Against Domestic Violence, on average, nearly twenty people per minute are physically abused by an intimate partner in the United States. In one year, this equates to more than 10 million women and men.

The cycle of violence that permeates every aspect of our lives is an existential and, in many cases, mortal threat to our shared humanity. Through it, we become conditioned to accept violence. Stigma comes from secrecy. In the pages that follow, I explore the steps that led to my becoming entangled in an abusive relationship, the roller coaster of coming forward, the aftermath, and my ongoing recovery. I also provide an appendix with resources for spotting intimate violence and getting help. By telling my story, I hope to help others to share their stories, to support loved ones in abusive relationships, and even to avoid becoming a victim.

I wish I didn't have memories of being a victim myself. No one wants such memories. But I feel that somehow the universe intended for me to encounter Eric Schneiderman and, eventually, end a cycle with his intimate partners that had been going on for a long time.

ASSUME NOTHING

THE FAIRY TALE

We met in July 2016 at the Democratic National Convention in Philadelphia. Producing election-related videos in 2016 was my first step into politics. It wasn't work I had sought to do, but when I was approached about the opportunity, I didn't hesitate. I wanted to get involved because I recognized the danger that the Republican candidate, Donald J. Trump, posed to the United States. As soon as he announced he was running, I thought, "This crook is going to win." I felt that if I didn't contribute to the effort to stop him, I wouldn't be able to sleep at night.

Prior to 2016, I had been more likely to be at an art opening, book signing, or theater show. It wasn't normal for me to attend large-scale political events, but that was about to change.

As for that first fateful encounter with Eric Schneiderman, I hadn't planned to be in the spot where he introduced himself to me. I hadn't planned to be at the convention at all that night.

After a long day producing a film shoot, I had wanted to stay in. But a series of unexpected events led to our meeting anyway.

It began with a text from a friend who was on the finance committee of Hillary Clinton's campaign. He had an extra pass. He was going to leave it with the receptionist at his hotel if I wanted it. I thought, "Why not?" Then, while on the subway, I received a message from a friend that he could see through Facebook that I was nearing the convention center. I texted him when I arrived, and he brought me to where he was sitting. It turned out to be the box of Ed Rendell, a former governor of Pennsylvania.

While I perched on a stool, taking notes, I could sense that a man was glancing at me. I turned to my right and smiled at him. I was wearing a cobalt blue dress with stars, a white vest, and red shoes. I must have looked like a proud American. He walked over.

"You're *writing* notes," he said, surprised.

Others around me were on their phones or laptops, but I preferred to use a notebook and pen.

Tim Kaine, the vice presidential candidate, was speaking. The man said he had gone to Harvard Law School with Kaine. I said that I had gone to Harvard for undergrad and grad.

"What did you study?"

"Chinese language and the history of law," I replied.

He asked, in Chinese, "Do you speak Chinese?"

I responded, in Chinese, "Yes, but I can't speak fluently anymore."

It was a charming and nerdy flirtation. He asked if I knew who he was. I did not.

"Where do you live?"

"New York," I said.

"Then I'm your lawyer."

He was surprised that I didn't know who he was. His name was Eric Schneiderman, and he was the attorney general of New York State.

After he rejoined his group, I found myself curious. I wanted to know more about him. He was older than the men I'd usually been interested in, but I thought he was handsome and smart. I loved the fact that he spoke Chinese. I wondered if I would see him again. I wanted to.

The next night, I was back at the convention and seated in a section high above the floor. I could see Eric on the jumbotron as the cameras panned over to where he stood with the New York delegation. I realized then that he was a big deal. During the proceedings, he and I emailed back and forth. We wouldn't see each other that night, but he said he would call me the next day. I decided to have no expectations. Maybe he would; maybe he wouldn't.

After the convention, I got a ride back to New York with Carrie Mae Weems, an artist I'd worked with for many years who had become a close friend. While we were in the car, he did in fact call. I felt butterflies. I was excited, and Carrie was excited for me, too. I was also impressed that he had done what he had said he was going to do. So many times, I had been disappointed by men not following through—not calling or canceling at the last minute, as if I had nothing better to do than wait for them. Eric and I made plans to meet for lunch the next day.

While I was in a postcall daze, Carrie asked, "What do you want?"

I responded, "I'm not sure. I don't know," which was accurate. I had not been in a relationship since my divorce almost two years before. I was in limbo but hopeful that I would meet someone. I was amazed that I had just met someone in real life.

When Eric and I got together, he came downtown so that it would be convenient for me, and he told his security detail that they didn't need to accompany us. He seemed nervous. After we sat down, he said abruptly, "I haven't vetted you yet." It seemed a strange thing to say right off the bat. I could feel a spark between us, but his comment took me out of the moment. I thought to myself, "Well, I've been vetted recently by the Hillary Clinton campaign."

That night I was leaving for Portland, Oregon, for three weeks. He was going to a meditation retreat upstate.

We stayed in contact through occasional emails, getting to know each other. He sent me articles about himself, one from the *American Prospect* about his being "the man the banks fear most" and one from the *Nation* that he wrote about "transforming the liberal checklist."

Once he emailed, "I am up in the woods with little reception, but will loop back in upon my return to the wheel of samsara. I hope you are well."

It was an optimistic time both in terms of our interactions with each other and in terms of the outlook for the election. But I was bewildered that he seemed interested in me. I didn't feel I looked like a politician's type. I looked too unconventional; I rarely got my hair done, and in my daily life, even at work, I could wear what I wanted. I wasn't the kind to be seen in monochromatic A-line dresses and pumps.

He emailed me when he was back in the city and sent a brief

about Exxon, with which he was engaged in a legal battle. He was a hero of the climate change movement. Two days later, he sent another article about himself and another battle, this one with Trump.

"Good fantasy reading before bed . . ." he wrote.

Although I could have been put off by his boasting, I saw it as a sign that he was trying to impress me. I felt flattered. I also felt that I could not reciprocate. What could I send him? An article on my book about my infertility struggles? A review of a downtown play I'd been in?

The night I returned to New York, he sent me yet another article about Exxon and wrote "Calling!" But I was at a friend's birthday dinner and told him I'd call afterward. For the next few days, he rang me every night, and we spoke for an hour or more. Then he asked me out to dinner.

He wanted to go to his favorite restaurant, Gabriel's, across the street from Jazz at Lincoln Center. I arrived before he did, and when I told the host whom I was meeting, I was immediately escorted to a prime booth, set apart from the tables in the middle of the space. When Eric got there, his favorite jazz song was playing. He was buoyant, almost dancing. During dinner, he joked about my being a spy sent by Exxon and said that the company had done a very good job. Soon, though, his expression grew dark, and he said, "You know, I could have your phone tapped." He also said he could have me followed. Was he trying to impress me? Was he trying to scare me? The moment passed in an instant, and I let it go. Otherwise, he was sweet and attentive, curious about my life and my work.

We didn't go home together. Later that night, he sent me another article about Exxon. He also sent me a photo of him with Ram Dass, the spiritual teacher and author of *Be Here Now.*

And he sent his "Transformational Activism Memo," which he said he had cowritten but which had been put out under the name of a friend, a meditation teacher. The memo provided a conceptual framework to "combine personal transformation with social and political activism aimed at transforming society."

At the time, I had taken a break from my paying jobs producing films, shows, and events to volunteer for the Clinton campaign by bringing artists and filmmakers together to create content to get out the vote. I had established a career as an arts and social justice organizer, beginning with my work for Anna Deavere Smith on the development of *Twilight: Los Angeles, 1992* about the human toll of the LA riots, and then with my serving on the steering committee of the NGO Forum/ Fourth World Conference on Women in Beijing, China, in 1995. Those were defining moments that had shaped the rest of my life. Eric's words about transformational activism resonated with me.

The following week, he invited me to join him in Amagansett, where a law school buddy had a home. He was waiting for me at the jitney bus stop wearing a blue short-sleeved polo shirt and jeans. I was wearing a summer dress with a watermelon print. I immediately felt as though we were on vacation together. Back at the house, we had separate but adjacent rooms. That night, after dinner, we made love. Then he wanted to look at the moonlight, so we went outside, onto the balcony. He brought out a portable speaker so we could dance. He held me gently and looked into my eyes as if he couldn't believe I was there.

The next day, he took me to two fund-raisers for Hillary Clinton in private homes. At the first one, everyone I met on Hillary's team seemed to know who I was. I took it as normal protocol that they had been briefed in advance about my background, specifically that I was volunteering as a producer of videos in support of the campaign. I was taken into a closed-off area where people were lined up to meet Hillary. When Eric and I finally got to her, she seemed keen to talk to him. After all, he was a great ally for keeping Trump in check. Moreover, if she won, Eric would be primed to play a central role in enacting her policies in New York State. Later, when she addressed the crowd, she name checked Eric and complimented him on the work he was doing.

At the second fund-raiser, Harvey Weinstein was one of the first people to approach Eric. He wanted to help him raise money, saying that Eric was "the only guy doing anything." I didn't know what to make of Weinstein. I had friends who worked for him. I had heard years before that he would make his assistants procure drugs and prostitutes for him when he was at film festivals. But here, at this event, he was doting on his young daughter.

Bill Clinton was seated near us. He told Eric he wanted to ask him something before he left. I spotted an acquaintance and wanted to say hello. Eric looked over at the woman and her husband, who were big philanthropists, and said, "Oh, they don't give me money." He didn't say it maliciously, but I gathered that at events like these, someone like him had to focus on his supporters—that he didn't have time for anyone else. I went to say hi to her anyway.

At the end of the night, Bill and Eric connected, and Eric

introduced me to the former president. Bill shook my hand firmly and didn't let it go. I almost started laughing as I processed a mix of thoughts. He could have been simply an aging man who had forgotten to let go of my hand. He could have been a typical politician trying to make me feel as though I mattered. It didn't feel sleazy, but the sexual misconduct allegations against him as well as his past friendships with notorious predators, such as Jeffrey Epstein and Ron Burkle, crossed my mind.

He asked Eric for advice about the Clinton Foundation and fund-raising, wanting to know when it needed to stop taking foreign donations. Eric gave him his card and said that someone in his office would help answer any questions. I was stunned by the overtness of the interaction. It was clear that Eric was an influential man.

A few days later, while we were still in Amagansett, Eric asked if I'd come home with him and spend the weekend at his place in the city. I said yes. He seemed genuinely interested in me, he seemed genuinely attracted to me, and I was swooning.

We drove straight from our minivacation to his home in a classic early-twentieth-century Upper West Side building that I associated with academics, families, and people who liked quiet surroundings. I lived on the opposite end of Manhattan, the Lower East Side, which was bustling with galleries, bars, and boutiques. Eric and I entered the grand lobby of his building, and a uniformed doorman greeted us. His apartment was large, with two bedrooms, three bathrooms, and a dining room with dark wood paneling. In the spacious living room was a painting of an old woman murkily rendered. It spooked me, but I didn't ask him about its significance.

On a dresser, he had a frame with the photo of him and Ram Dass. He told me the photo had been taken by a previous girlfriend. She was one of several women he described as crazy "shark women," who he believed dated him only because of his powerful position. He mentioned his ex-wife, who continued to serve as his adviser; he referred to her as a "stone-cold killer." He said he had never met anyone like me. He made me feel different and also separate from the women before me.

He looked at the scars on my body and with sympathetic eyes told me he admired my ability to overcome adversity. (In May 2012, I had had surgery to remove two cancers, a thymoma and a gastrointestinal stromal tumor [GIST].) I said that there were many people who had dealt with far more adversity than I would ever know.

"You're a good turnip," he said in a sincere tone. He had already come up with an affectionate nickname for me, based on the title of my website, Tanya Turns Up. It was a nickname I had gotten in college because I was known for turning up to support my friends at their events.

My scars had long been a source of insecurity for me. A scar runs down the length of my torso in three parts. It starts above my heart and pauses near the center of my rib cage. There is a small mark where a chest tube was. The scar resumes below my navel and ends at the top of my pelvic bone. On the one hand, I think they are very punk rock, thin, jagged lines that separate the left and right sides of my body. On the other hand, they are a visible marker of the year I had been ill.

In the fall of 2012, a few months after my surgery, my former husband told me he wanted to separate. We were in France, on tour with a show that he was directing and I had produced and also appeared in. His announcement came on the heels of a trying few years during which I had endured three miscarriages and an attempt at fertility treatment that was abruptly cut short when the tumors were discovered. Instead of making a new life, I had been obliged to save my own.

I started writing *The Big Lie* while I was in the midst of pursuing fertility treatment. I was shaken by how many friends and friends of friends had stories to tell, too, about their own experiences with infertility and their lack of in-depth fertility awareness. I decided to aggregate what I was learning and speak to experts about what they wished more people knew.

By the time I turned in the manuscript, my life had taken so many twists and turns, with the surgery to remove the tumors and my marital problems, that even my editor was surprised by what he read.

When I wasn't working on the book, I was on my knees with grief, mourning the loss of a life I had thought would last the rest of my days. I thought maybe it would come back. My former husband was not making any moves to pursue divorce; he made it seem as if he just needed to figure things out. But a year later, at my book release party, a woman who had worked with both of us revealed that my husband had actually been in a relationship with his assistant director. Many of my friends had warned me about her. They had thought she was angling to take my place. One even said, "She wants your life." But I had dismissed their concerns. I had never felt jealous. Besides, at that time, she had been in a relationship with another woman.

I think it was the day after my book party that I contacted a lawyer and pushed forward with getting a divorce. If he had moved on, I needed to as well. I didn't think my husband was a bad person. He had just done a bad thing. There were times that I felt he could have killed me with the timing of his actions. But it was liberating to know the truth. I focused on my recovery and chose not to feel any bitterness.

That was the beginning of the next phase of my life. I started spending more time in Portland, Oregon, where my best friend from college lived. I visited him there at least once a year. Portland is my happy place, where my shoulders instantly relax as soon as the plane touches down at the airport.

It took me a while after my divorce to feel that I could even look at a man in a sexual way. I felt nervous when there was just an inkling of attraction. I had scars on my torso that hadn't been there when I had met my ex-husband. I thought they might unnerve men if I took my clothes off; I thought my body looked like that of a sick person. Also, my husband had said he wanted to separate after, not before, I had the scars.

One of the more hurtful things my ex had said to justify his leaving was that he had been going along with the relationship, that what we had been were simply great business partners (though, he added, "passionate ones"). Everything I had thought to be real about us was not. I felt as though I had been duped by someone who had been using me in many ways.

By the time I met Eric, I felt that I was ready to be with someone again. His values seemed to align with mine. He was worshipped by those around him. He seemed as though he would be a good boyfriend. At the time, I believed he was the opposite of my ex. What primarily attracted me to Eric were his overt claims that he was transformational rather than transactional.

The week after spending that first weekend at his place, I

went to New Haven, Connecticut, to work with Carrie Mae Weems on her show at the Yale Repertory Theatre. The show was *Grace Notes: Reflections for Now,* and I was the associate director. It addressed the cycle of violence against black people, called for an end to violence, and commemorated black lives lost since the election of President Barack Obama.

While I was away, Eric called often. Carrie said, "He's the attorney general of New York State. He's got this much god-damned time to call you?" One night, while Carrie and I were going home from the theater, during the twenty-minute walk, she said, "He's called you three times since we left the theater. If my husband called me that many times, I'd hang up on him." She continued, "I see aspects that he's trying to control you." I didn't grasp the insight of her words. I didn't see Eric's atten-tion as threatening. I felt that he deeply missed me.

Eric sent me songs via email: "The Way You Look Tonight" and "You'd Be So Nice to Come Home To."

What an unexpected turn of events in my life. After my di-vorce, I had thought that eventually I would meet someone, but I hadn't foreseen that that person would be the attorney general of New York State, a political rising star, and a very powerful man.

ENTRAP

On his desk at home was a copy of *Dark Money: The Hidden History of the Billionaires Behind the Rise of the Radical Right*, by Jane Mayer. On the bookshelf in his office at 120 Broadway was a copy of *Life on the Outside: The Prison Odyssey of Elaine Bartlett*, by Jennifer Gonnerman, a longtime friend of mine. I believed they were good omens.

I attended a talk Eric was giving with two meditation teachers. The theme was the relationship between spirituality and social engagement, how to stay aligned during the turbulent times before the election.

Looking back, I see how I got sucked in. His outward-facing spirituality was a mask for the torment beneath the surface. His outward-facing feminism was a mask for his misogyny. Through public events like the one that night, he perpetuated a narrative of himself as an agent of change and transformation. Many people I trusted depicted him as a hero, and he positioned himself as standing up for many causes I believed in. I bought it.

In between college and law school, Eric had worked at a clinic that provided abortions. He had given women rides from the airport to the clinic and comforted them. He had been a deputy sheriff in the Berkshires and befriended prisoners there. He showed me a letter that an inmate had written him, thanking him for his kindness. He frequently told a story about how the New York State GOP had tried to cut him out of the state senate by reshaping his district to be mostly Dominican, knowing he didn't speak Spanish. So he had taught himself Spanish, pounded the pavement within the newly drawn lines, and won. He introduced me to many of his allies in the Latinx community. When I went with him to have dinner with a Dominican American congressperson, Eric seemed proud to show me off. I went from feeling that I was not the typical politician's girlfriend to feeling that my being brown was an asset to his ambitions; he often talked about running for governor one day.

He made a concerted effort to support me in my world. He came to an Artists for Hillary gathering in Brooklyn that I had helped put together, and he spoke to the group. He came to pick me up from the campaign headquarters after I had a meeting there. But I also realized that my world at the time provided him with a personal connection to the campaign. It was something I could add to his profile. If only I could have seen how horribly wrong everything would go, both politically and personally—the negativity and chaos in one sphere influenced the other.

But it wouldn't be fair to assert that our relationship was only about what I could do for him. It also made sense in the context of the work we were both engaged in. And perhaps most important, there was tenderness and camaraderie between us. There was communication. I felt that he wanted to be a good boyfriend. Many of my friends thought he was a catch. They also thought I was in for a wild ride, with a front-row seat to the national political theater.

Soon after we began dating, he took me to the wedding of a congressman's son. We were seated with a politician I happened to know. He was surprised to see me with Eric and said something to the effect that it was good for Eric but maybe not for me. He said it jokingly, but in retrospect, I wondered if there was something behind that comment. That same month, Eric took me to the Global Citizen Festival in Central Park, where we were escorted onstage and stood in the wings. Metallica was playing. I found it funny that Eric didn't know who they were.

Eric and I were becoming more enmeshed. As a producer and artist, I went to my share of galas and openings, but when I attended high-profile events with Eric, I was "the girlfriend." I felt elevated in terms of clout but diminished in terms of my own achievements.

Despite that, I enjoyed being his regular companion at intimate dinners with politicians and important donors and at outings to Jazz at Lincoln Center, his favorite venue. I love hearing live music, and getting to meet the artists through Eric was especially exciting: going backstage to say hi to Joey Alexander, the young Indonesian jazz piano prodigy, and Wynton Marsalis. I enjoyed attending each other's events and cheering each other on; talking openly and honestly about our hopes and fears; dancing around his apartment.

Still, other patterns were emerging. He often asked me to make connections for him, for fund-raising, for volunteers. I didn't think much of the requests at the time; a lot of people asked me for favors. But he seemed to be interested in my friends only if they could be of some use to him. When we had dinner with friends of mine, he appeared uninterested in hearing about their lives. He seemed to want to talk only about himself and what he was doing as attorney general. He sometimes referred to my friends as "ditzes" or "clueless"—but they were very intelligent women.

When I later read Beverly Engel's book *The Emotionally Abusive Relationship: How to Stop Being Abused and How to Stop Abusing*, I learned about the connection between narcissistic personality disorder (NPD)—which I believe Eric displayed— and abusive behavior. Engel wrote, "Those with NPD are often oblivious to others and how their behavior affects them." She also explained that "too much closeness terrifies a narcissistic individual and so he criticizes or imposes control on his partner to hold her at bay."

Politicians have to be charismatic so that when they say "Jump," people ask "How high?" Abusers are often charismatic, too. Politicians and abusers can share another characteristic: extreme narcissism.

At first, Eric was so adoring and supportive of me that I didn't pick up on his extreme narcissism, such as when he emailed me article after article about himself. Also, if the outcome of the election was going to be as all the pundits predicted, he would be more prominent than ever, and I would be by his side. After more than two decades of working with arts and social justice organizations, I could bring my skills to a larger platform, and for him, having a girl-friend like me could enhance his profile. I was feeling an adrenaline rush from the romance and headiness of my new relationship.

3

ISOLATE

On Election Day, November 8, 2016, I rolled out of bed in my apartment on the Lower East Side and voted in my building, which was a polling center. At the time, I was still on social media. I scrolled through photo after photo of people excited that the United States might finally have a female president after nearly a century of women having the right to vote. Women posted photos of themselves holding their daughters with the caption "I VOTED FOR HER." I myself posted a photo in which I held a Hillary sign after voting. I wore a white pantsuit for the occasion.

I had already begun talking with campaign staffers about ideas for the inauguration. I proposed having women heads of state from around the world record congratulatory messages for Hillary, acknowledging her historic moment. Eric was similarly brimming with confidence about the outcome.

He and I had a full night of viewing parties and celebrations to attend. I put on a new, bright pink, knee-length cape dress and heels. I preferred to wear boots, flats, or sneakers, but Eric always wanted me in heels at events. I paid to have my hair done because he always wanted me to wear my hair up or blown straight. Otherwise, he often said my hair looked too wild. Perhaps he meant it looked too ethnic. My hair is wavy, bordering on frizzy when it's humid. The bigger it gets, the more I like it. I thought, "What is wrong with my natural hair?" Also, getting my hair done felt like a waste of time, and I didn't enjoy the process of having my hair pulled and flattened. But Eric made me feel insecure about my hair. If I didn't conform, I wouldn't be pretty in his eyes.

First we went to a party hosted by Harvey Weinstein at Cipriani Downtown, but we left after a short time to get to our next stop, a party uptown hosted by George Soros. By the time we arrived, the tide was already turning for the worse, and a somber cloud was descending. We soon made our way to the Javits Center, where it felt as though everyone was on a sinking ship. Eric and I were taken to a VIP area, where many celebrities were in tears on couches and on the floor as they watched televisions. The main hall teemed with people in a state of paralysis. I found a quiet corner where I called a journalist friend who was covering the election. She told me it was over, based on the results that were coming in. An outdated Electoral College, voter suppression and manipulation, and false information spread by Facebook were going to result in the bad guys winning. We had been pretending that we lived in a democracy.

A day that had started with boundless promise was ending in utter devastation, not just for me but for the majority of

Americans. The existential threat that Trump's candidacy had posed to the country was coming to pass. The misogyny and racism he embodied would be unleashed.

A little before midnight, Eric and I went home, though the winner had not yet been announced. We received call after call from friends and colleagues seeking comfort. I felt that whatever the outcome, now our real work had to begin.

The next morning, when I emerged from his apartment, a gray pall seemed to hang over the streets. Most people looked gray, too, as if the life force were being sucked out of them. We lived in the city that had built Trump, a city that had allowed him to cannibalize it for his personal profit. We were confronted by his name on buildings throughout the city.

Here was a man who at every opportunity had stoked the worst impulses of humankind. Take, for example, his behavior during the Central Park jogger case, a violent rape that had torn the city apart in 1989. The following year, five innocent black and brown boys had been wrongly convicted of the crime, and Trump had played an outsize part in convincing the public that they were guilty. He had taken out full-page newspaper ads calling for the death penalty. Eventually, the five boys had been exonerated, but by then their lives had been destroyed and degraded. Trump, predictably, has never apologized or shown remorse.

I happened to have friends who knew people with disturbing stories about him, such as a woman he had dated who had supposedly been forbidden to touch his hair or use his bathroom and who had been told to avoid being photographed with him because she was a woman of color. One person told me the story about his close friend who had lived in a building that Trump had bought. Attempting to force the tenants to leave, Trump had deployed ruthless tactics with the help of a new management agency, which had cut off the heat and hot water and let garbage pile up to attract rodents. Tales of Trump's nefarious and insidious behavior were well known in New York circles.

Because of his previous legal battles with Trump, Eric was in a position to defend New York against the Trump administration. He spent the day after the election consoling his staff and strategizing for the future. He started rallying Democratic attorneys general around the country to prepare for the attacks on civil liberties and vulnerable communities that were sure to come. Meanwhile, I felt at a loss. I had really hoped that after the election, I would be able to sail off into the sunset and get back to the work I had been doing previously. I could reconnect with the artists and organizations I had collaborated with for years and explore new opportunities. I thought that my work with US politics would be done. But for the moment, I had to continue. Also, I was now a politician's girlfriend, and I threw myself into the role.

I started a newsletter that highlighted how people could get involved and offered words of inspiration. I was sorry that the United States was about to experience a period of great tumult, but it wouldn't be the first such period, and I felt we would come out on the other side. I drew on what I knew about my birth country. For decades, Sri Lanka had endured a brutal civil war that had claimed tens of thousands of lives, including that of my paternal grandmother. It had also had its share of autocratic rulers, under which the country had become one of the most dangerous in the world for journalists.

My parents had brought me from Sri Lanka to the United States when I was a toddler, but I had always felt a strong connection to the land. I have a large extended family there; my mother was one of eight siblings. Except for when the war was especially bad in the 1980s, I would visit as much as I could for holidays and family occasions.

Eric went with me to Sri Lanka for Christmas. It greatly impressed my relatives that such an important person would make the exhausting journey to the other end of the world. During our visit, he was the most relaxed I had ever seen him. Even though the election had gone terribly wrong just a month before, he was now in a country that was very far away. He talked about how everything looked and smelled different. We would go for walks at the Galle Fort by the Indian Ocean. I took him scuba diving, and he said it was the best dive he had ever done. On Christmas Day, he helped my grandmother, with her two deteriorated hips, walk up the stairs of her home. He sat and talked with her.

But the darkness was starting to seep in; his need to isolate me from my family and friends was increasing. One day at my grandmother's house, where all my family were assembled, he turned to me suddenly and said, "I can't take much more of this."

I took it to mean he didn't want to be around my family anymore. I had come all this way to see them, but I told him he could do his own thing. The next day, he stayed at the hotel while I went to family gatherings.

Before we left Sri Lanka, my aunt organized an elaborate dinner for us. She made sure to have enough vegetables and fish because I told her Eric didn't eat meat. My family does eat

meat, though, and there was a chicken dish. I am not a vege-
tarian, but he wouldn't allow me to eat meat in his presence. He
saw me looking at the dish and glanced at me disapprovingly.

After we returned to the United States, I felt another series
of dark pivots in our relationship. By that point, I was essentially living with him. I had gradually taken more and more
of my belongings from my apartment to his place. We talked
about possibly staying at my place some nights, spending a
weekend downtown, but he said it would take too much co-
ordination because of his need for security. My building had
twenty-four-hour guards, and I told him he could have his own
security detail outside. But that didn't make a difference. We
never stayed at my place.

I missed my life downtown, the ease of contact with my
support network of friends and collaborators, but he didn't
want me out of his sight. On one occasion, I was at a film event
in Tribeca. It was pouring rain, and I was near my place. I left
him a message that I was sorry, but I was going to stay downtown.

When I was a few blocks away from my house, he phoned,
shouting at me, "I can't trust you!" A friend who was walking beside me looked alarmed. She could hear his angry tone
through the phone. I felt embarrassed that she was witnessing
the exchange. But I didn't know how to address it with her, and
we just kept walking. I let the moment pass.

Another time, I was receiving an award from a vocational
training program for women of color. As the event ended, Eric
called to say that he had landed unexpectedly early from Al-
bany and needed dinner. He didn't ask me how the event had
gone. He didn't congratulate me. He wanted me to leave right
away and pick up food for him.

Later, my friend who had gone with me to the event would admit that she could hear his tone through the phone, and it had freaked her out. She had thought, "How dare he? She's not his slave. I don't care who he is." She had been so troubled that she had gone home and told her husband but had decided not to say anything to me.

Meanwhile, I was ignoring the signs. I felt that I was the one making mistakes.

One day, I went with a friend to see a Broadway show. She's like my sister, someone I can tell anything to. She asked how Eric was doing, and I said something to the effect of "There's a lot going on." She said, "You seem subdued in the relationship." Later, when I finally confided in her, she would say she wished she had asked more questions and read between the lines.

One night, Eric and I had dinner with a friend of mine from college and her husband. Later, that friend told me that she had noticed how possessive he was of me; she had noticed how much he drank; she had noticed his narcissism; and although she thought he clearly loved me, she said it seemed as though his love acted as a validation for him. Another friend, when she met him, said she noticed how willing he was to objectify me into his life. The focus was always on him. He didn't talk about me at all and seemed interested in my life only as it served him.

After the election, his drinking started to acquire an increasingly dark undertone. As he became more comfortable with me, the addictions started to spill out; having me close to him was both a mirror and a crutch. I would wake up to find that he had eaten my yogurt directly from the container because he was hungry in the middle of the night after taking Ambien and lorazepam along with alcohol. Sometimes I would wake up to find him staggering around the apartment, and I would guide him back to bed.

When he was sober, I would sometimes describe to him his behavior during the night. His face would show regret and distress. I felt sorry for him because his pain was so deep that he was trying to annihilate himself. But I started to realize that he was trying to annihilate me, too. There was a growing dissonance between the man who cared deeply about me and the dark man who wanted to obliterate himself and take me down with him.

He manipulated me by giving me things and then taking them away. Because he wanted me in his space, he offered me the guest room to use as my own. But he wouldn't let me put a desk in it so that I could have a study. I worked on the living room couch or at the dining table, until he got annoyed that I was working in those areas. Eventually he said I could use his office, which he never used himself. But the Wi-Fi didn't work there because the room was far from the router. He kept confining me to narrower spaces while accusing me of taking up too much space. He wouldn't let me install a second closet in the guest room, so my clothes were squeezed into a small space until eventually he let me hang some items in his closet.

One day, I was handwashing clothes in the guest bathroom. As I hung them up to dry, he walked over from the master bedroom, and asked, "What are you doing?"

I replied with amusement, "Handwashing my fine lingerie."

He said with annoyance, "It looks like Chinatown."

I felt as though I couldn't move without committing an offense.

Meanwhile, he was constantly asking me to listen to him

practice his speeches and to work with his staff on inviting people to his fund-raisers. He never showed gratitude and sometimes belittled how much I helped him, even though he seemed
dependent on me. He would also accuse me of not creating
enough separation between his work and our relationship, even
when he was the one asking for my help.

Still, there were times when he was present and positive.
He talked about our moving into a bigger apartment so that I
could have my own proper study. He talked about our having
children. That made me laugh. I would ask, "Do you have any
idea what my first book was about?" *The Big Lie* had been about
my infertility.

In January 2017, two nights before the presidential inauguration, I stayed at my place because I was supposed to speak at
an event downtown the next day. In the morning, I got a call
from him. He was in an emergency room. He told me he had
drunk too much the night before and fallen in the bathroom.
When he had woken up, he was lying in a pool of blood. His
security detail had had to take him to the hospital. I asked if he
wanted me to come. He said yes. On the way to the hospital,
I called the event organizer and told her I was sorry, but I had
to cancel my talk.

When I arrived at the hospital, I saw how badly he had been
bruised. He had a black eye and stitches around his eyebrow.
He was scheduled to do a press conference later that day. I told
him he couldn't; his injury was too obvious and would elicit
questions. He asked me to take a photo and send it to his communications person, which I did. In addition to his communications person, he talked with his ex-wife, with whom he still
regularly consulted. After speaking with them, he said I was

to tell anyone who asked that he had fallen while jogging—a curious explanation, since he rarely jogged.

What goes on in the house, I had learned, stays in the house. In some ways, that felt normal to me. When I was a child, I had grown accustomed to keeping family secrets, about the violence between my parents. Here with Eric, the cone of silence was closing in. If I betrayed it, I would be jeopardizing not only his career but also the service that he was doing for the country. How would it look if the attorney general of New York State had been so drunk the night before the inauguration that he had ended up in the hospital? Back at his apartment, where the murky portrait of the old woman seemed to glare at me as I entered, I tried my best to clean up the bloodstains that were all over the bedroom.

He had already made me feel trapped at home. Now he was gradually isolating me from the world outside. It wasn't just his substance abuse I had to hide; I was also being more frequently exposed to encounters that shouldn't have happened in my presence. I felt he was being careless, having work conversations I shouldn't have overheard. On some occasions, he said if we broke up he would have to kill me. Sometimes he would pose it as a question.

One night, we were in the dining room standing by the head of the long, dark, wooden table. He was showing me old photos and letters, including from his time as a sheriff. Suddenly he paused and asked, "Am I going to have to kill you if we break up?"

I didn't react; I didn't say anything to respond to or make light of what he said. Instead, I filed his words away in my mind. Such moments passed quickly. Later, they would add up.

Numerous times, when we were together in public, people approached him as if he were the Second Coming. They would say "Save us." Occasionally, people in government or with close ties to government officials would call him or meet with him, offering what they claimed was inside intelligence on the current administration. They thought he was their best shot at delivering the United States from the clutches of a dangerous president. Even the president himself sent an envoy, one of his personal lawyers, to deliver a message to Eric: that he was sorry for the clashes they'd had in the past and hopeful that they could find common ground. He also wanted Eric to know that he was not really a Republican.

That's how powerful Eric was.

I began to think to myself, "If only they knew what a mess Eric is at home. If only they knew what he does to me."

Those exchanges added to my increasing disaffection with politics. Every politician and member of his or her inner circle, I was coming to see, was in collusion with one another; no one was who he or she pretended to be. They all had something on one another, and they protected one another. They cared only about power and who got to wield it. They didn't care about the people.

I was caught up in a confusing labyrinth, and I couldn't talk to anyone about it.

4

CONTROL

Often, when he looked at my chest, Eric would tell me to see his plastic surgeon and get rid of my scars. In the early days of our relationship, he had spoken about my scars as if they were a badge of courage. He also suggested that I get a boob job and get into shape. He made me think, "If I want to be the first lady, I have to change how I look."

Soon after Eric and I began dating, Carrie Mae Weems asked, "My God, Tanya, what are you going to wear? Do you have to get a whole new wardrobe?"

A friend told me about her experience dating a future senator and presidential candidate while they were in college. When he had broken up with her, he had said, "You're not first lady material." For men with political ambitions, the way their partner looks impacts their prospects. In my situation, Eric's controlling of my appearance was a thread in a larger web of manipulation.

As his interest in meditation and Buddhism had grown,

so had his interest in reconnecting with the faith of his birth: Judaism. He attended a synagogue in his neighborhood and started taking me with him. He told me stories about how Jared Kushner and Ivanka Trump had, years before, tried to befriend him. After all, as the attorney general of New York State, he had jurisdiction over their families' businesses. When the three of them had gotten together, they had bonded over their commitment to Judaism. Ivanka, Eric said, was well versed in the teachings of the faith.

Jared and Ivanka would eventually become Eric's enemies, especially after he initiated the fraud case against Trump University. At the time, Jared was the publisher of the *New York Observer* and printed a front-page story about Eric with an illustration depicting him as the sinister Malcolm McDowell character from the film *A Clockwork Orange*.

I consider myself agnostic, leaning toward atheist, but I didn't mind going with Eric to synagogue. I've attended places of worship of many denominations and recognize that congregating with others in a religious community provides people with comfort and purpose. One night, Eric asked if I would consider converting. He said he would even take the classes with me. He wanted to draw me closer into his orbit.

However, he seemed uncomfortable when he was in mine. On my birthday, I was giving a talk about women's activism. Many friends attended. He came, too, which I thought was a wonderful gesture because he was busy with his own events. Toward the end of the evening, my friends gathered around and a cake was brought out. But soon afterward, he insisted that we leave immediately. My friends couldn't believe that he was making me leave my own birthday celebration. One later told me that his behavior was "jarring."

His forcing me to leave my own events happened on a number of occasions, including at a fund-raiser I organized for him. A friend stood patiently by my side, waiting to meet him after he finished talking with another guest, but he suddenly said we had to leave. I told him I wanted him to meet my friend. He gave me an agitated look and hurried me toward the door. My friend tried to walk with us, to have at least a few words with him.

She said, "I want to know who this person is who has won my friend's heart."

He couldn't have cared less. He looked at her blankly, opened the door to the car, and motioned for me to get in. Afterward, she told another friend, "I don't like him. Tanya can't be herself around him."

He didn't like me talking on the phone, even though he was often on the phone himself. If he heard me on the phone in another room with the door closed, he would come, open the door, glare at me, and shake his head. I would try to wrap up the call quickly.

During one call with my mother, she said, "You get very quiet when he's around. My friends notice when I try to talk to you."

And there was his preventing me from eating certain foods. During Fashion Week 2017, we went to a dinner party at a sprawling loft in SoHo, hosted by a designer we had met through one of Eric's biggest donors. The date coincided with Valentine's Day. I knew it would be a fancy crowd, so I tried to be fashionable. I wore a black turtleneck and vintage white

Courrèges pants that I had bought at a store in the East Village. In black boots with heels, I was standing tall, as uniformed waiters came by with plates of beautifully arranged hors d'oeuvres. One came by with a chicken dish. I really wanted to eat it, but because Eric was there, I didn't. He glared at me and, out of earshot of anyone else, said, "I saw the way you were looking at that."

Another time, we were having dinner at a seafood restaurant on the Upper West Side. Complimentary chocolate pudding was served at the end of the meal. Chocolate pudding is one of my favorite desserts. Eric wasn't eating his, so after I finished mine, I asked if I could have the second one. The cup was quite small. He looked at me as though I were a naughty child and said, "Bad turnip." I felt as though I couldn't eat sweets and couldn't eat meat with him around. I cherished the nights I met friends for dinner. Whether I was in the mood for meat or dessert or not, I ordered both.

Eric's need to subjugate me extended to our sexual interactions. When he first slapped me in the face while we were making love, it happened in the blink of an eye. No man had ever done that to me. He seemed to be testing me. I didn't know what to do. I tried to make sense of it. We had been dating for about six weeks, and I thought of him as a meditator, someone who espoused spirituality and who fought on behalf of vulnerable people. At that moment, I became aware that he could inflict great harm on me.

Over time, the slaps got harder and began to be accompanied by demands. In bed, he would slap me until I agreed to find him a young girl for a three-way. I told him what he wanted to hear even though I knew it was never going to happen. He would slap me until I agreed to call him "Master" or "Daddy." He recounted his fantasies of finding me somewhere far away to be his slave, his "brown girl."

I wondered what he called his previous girlfriends. The ones I was aware of were white. With me, he said I had "wild" hair and unsightly scars, and he wanted me to be his slave. Publicly, he was a friend and ally to communities of color; he was a big supporter and fan of jazz artists. But in the bedroom, he wanted to be "Master" and slap around his "slave."

He would hurl spit into my mouth and mash his lips against mine so that it was hard for me to breathe. A few times, he put his hands around my throat and tried to choke me. When I tried to move his hands, he ordered me to let go. I would say, "Hey, that hurts." I would tell him to stop. But he didn't respond to my protests. Each time, he looked at me as if he were possessed, and then the moment quickly passed. I felt as if I had vertigo. I was scared.

I didn't realize it at the time, but I was dealing with the kind of abuse that can go on between people in committed relationships: intimate violence. But I had convinced myself that he would be my partner, maybe for life. If I wanted to keep him, I felt I had to let him dominate me.

I tolerated the situation because it was disorienting and so disconnected from the person he presented in public. By day, he was the crusading attorney general, and he had to be nimble and sober. At night, as soon as he got home, he would start swigging from a bottle, usually wine but sometimes vodka. I tried to get him to pour it into a glass so he could keep track of how much he was consuming. He would pour me a glass of bourbon and push it toward me, saying "Drink your bourbon, turnip."

But watching the way he drank at home made me not want to drink myself. He took the joy out of having a drink to wind down at the end of the night. He made me feel as if I had to be his caretaker in case he drank too much. He would take Ambien and lorazepam at the same time. I reminded him that the combination of those drugs and alcohol make people do crazy things.

Sometimes I was woken up by the sound of him watching movies or television beside me in bed, with the volume up loud. He liked to watch *Sneaky Pete*, *The Americans*, and clips from late-night talk shows. I would say that I needed to rest and maybe I should sleep in the guest room, which made him upset. Other times, I would be woken up by his fingers inside me or his hands squeezing parts of my body. He seemed to be moving in his sleep and would say things like "I love you" or "My bad, bad girl, Daddy's going to rape you." I remember on a few occasions, after he had passed out, going to the guest room and sitting down with tears rolling down my cheeks.

He started asking me to hide the bottles from him. I took the task seriously but found it increasingly difficult to find a hiding place he wouldn't discover—under the couch, behind the television, nowhere seemed safe. And then I thought, "I'll put the vodka bottle deep in my bag of dirty laundry. He'll never find it. He wouldn't be that gross, would he?"

But in the morning, the bottle was empty.

He said smugly, "You didn't do your job."

Mornings were hard for him. He would struggle to wake up. He would brush me away with a hand gesture if I tried to be near him. He would stagger around the apartment in a daze.

He would drink cup after cup of coffee, trying to shake off the night before.

I longed for signs of affection and intimacy. When we had those moments, I was happy with him, lying on the couch in an embrace as he played me his favorite songs. I tolerated the times when we had sex and he slapped me and spat at me, calling me his property and his brown slave. I thought, "I can put up with that much." As long as the abuse wasn't happening the majority of the time—maybe one day a week—I was able to compartmentalize it. That was how I coped with the situation. But I began to realize that I was in an endless cycle of abuse.

He made me feel that he needed me, and I felt empathy for his difficult childhood. His parents had gone through a bitter divorce, and because they didn't want anything to do with each other, they had neglected him. I could feel the loneliness that he had carried with him throughout his life. Many times, he would look into my eyes and ask, "Are you going to take care of me?"

I wanted to love him completely. For a while, I did. I also bought into the notion of us: as he rose in his field, I thought, I would rise with him. He would say, "We're a good team." We could accomplish so much together. We could help change the world. But he was Dr. Jekyll and Mr. Hyde, and I never knew which would be dominant—especially at night, when he was drinking.

When things were bad, I dissociated. I thought the situation would calm down, that he would change. I thought the good side would win. But I had never seen someone I was in a relationship with so out of control and dependent on uppers and downers. A few times, he acknowledged that he needed help, but he was worried that if he got it, the world would find out. There had to be a shroud of silence around the subject. I encouraged him to at least talk to a therapist. I had him speak on the phone with mine. I connected them by email, and they set up a time to talk one evening. I was in the apartment when they spoke, but I couldn't hear the conversation because Eric was in another room with the door closed. After fifteen minutes, he emerged, having ended the call, and said he was fine.

In February, about a month after Eric landed in the hospital, I had lunch with a director friend, and I admitted that things were not going well. I told her that Eric was depressed and I was trying to help him. She had been with us at a dinner with filmmakers who wanted to make a documentary about him. But in the weeks since they had first approached him and his team about the idea, I had become concerned that Eric could be so un-self-aware as to think having cameras follow him around wouldn't be a disastrous idea. I told my friend that I didn't think Eric should be part of the documentary. Later, after the *New Yorker* story, she reached out to me and said she'd realized she could have read between the lines.

There were also times when *I* was the one not reading between the lines, when people tried to warn me. When I first started seeing Eric, a friend and mentor tried to tell me over dinner, "I want you to be careful. I've heard—" The waiter arrived, and she didn't finish the thought after he left. A year later, as I started to write down for myself every bit of pain that I had experienced with him, I reached out to my friend and asked if she remembered what she had wanted to tell me.

Without hesitation, she said, "Yes, I heard he has a reputation for using and abusing women, then discarding them."

Another friend told me that she had been worried when I had confided in her early on about his drinking. Later, when I told her that he slapped and spat at me without my consent almost every time we had sex, she was shocked but not surprised.

I always wondered if he had done the same to his previous girlfriends and sexual partners, but I thought the abuse was specific to me. He told me he'd never been with anyone like me. He praised my activism and my work, but he demeaned and humiliated me as a person.

The darkness increasingly seeped into our daytime and non-sexual interactions through his criticisms and need to control me. On many occasions, I told him that I felt he was trying to ruin my self-esteem. He said he was depressed. The times were turbulent; he was going to work on himself. He prayed and meditated. Sometimes we meditated together, and in those moments, I felt hopeful and at ease with him. But his spiritual practice was not enough to reconcile the conflict between what he said and what he did, between his daytime and late-night behavior.

I meditate every morning. It's a practice I began when I was sick. During those fifteen minutes, when my thoughts wander, I mine my memory for connections between my past and my present. I've made many mistakes, but I am essentially the woman I wanted to be: I went to graduate school. I'm an artist and producer. For my whole career, I have been working with women's and social justice organizations.

I grew up around domestic violence. In my earliest memory, I am clutching a stuffed bunny as I stand in the living room, crying at the top of my lungs, watching my father—who towers over my mother by almost a foot—with his hands raised. I must have been three years old. At one point my father kicks my mother. They are cursing each other. He calls her a bitch; she calls him a shit. The fights usually happened at night, as if both of them had alter egos that came out after dark. My father, a psychiatrist, had encountered many split personalities—how was it, I sometimes wonder, that he never conquered his own? Yet at the same time, as a child, I watched *Superman*. I was Wonder Woman on many Halloweens, and my favorite doll was the Bionic Woman. It's human, I suppose, to want to be two people.

I am terrified by the memory of my father beating my mother. But I also remember how much I loved the stuffed bunny in my hand.

A few years later, after we moved from an apartment in downtown Los Angeles to a big house in Long Beach, about an hour away, I rushed into my parents' bedroom in the middle of the night. I had heard screams; I had heard those now-familiar curse words. I was maybe eight years old. My father again towered above my mother, but this time I was tall, too. I grabbed his hands and held them tightly so he couldn't beat her.

One day in the kitchen, my father put a knife into my hand and told me in an anguished voice, "Kill me. Why don't you just kill me?"

I stayed quiet. He walked away. I stared at the knife.

One night in my room, he sat down beside me on the bed and started sobbing.

I know he loved me, but he seemed so broken so many times. As I got older, the beatings became less frequent, because

I was there to witness them and restrain my father. One day, when he attempted to beat my mother, before I could intervene, she called the cops. But she had me to police him, so I couldn't see what she could achieve by this except to bring shame, not just on my father but on all of us. Now we had an "incident" on record. The cops stood at the door of my bedroom, attempting to ask me questions, but I wondered what good it would do to answer. I was watching television—*Land of the Lost*, a series about a family that travels back in time to the age of the dinosaurs—and I was happy to be in another universe. I heard my mother say to them, "She doesn't want to get married because of what she sees with me."

Was that true? Was that what my mother believed?

I used to avoid discussing those memories, not because they were painful but because I felt they tainted me. Perhaps my own experience with intimate partner violence is what has propelled me to write this and make more sense of my memories.

In Margaret Atwood's introduction to *The Handmaid's Tale*, she wrote about "the Dear Reader for whom every writer writes." The act of writing is hopeful because it implies that there is a reader, the Dear Reader, out there. The Dear Reader is also the writer's future self; the writer can later refer to what has been written. The Dear Reader is someone who, like me, might have clutched her stuffed animal for comfort during difficult times.

As I reveal my memories now, I know I am a child from an abusive household. How has that scarred me in ways I cannot see? My childhood made me stronger: As a teenager, I resolved to be happy. I resolved never to put up with abuse. But I know I love my father. He was in all other roles—father, doctor, friend—a generous and compassionate man. I cannot reconcile his abuse of my mother with his good attributes, but I forgive him.

When I saw my father hit my mother, I stood up to him. I looked up divorce lawyers in the phone book and made an appointment for my mother. Still, abuse happened to me. What I experienced as an adult, in my forties, felt different from what I witnessed as a child. My father had given my mother a black eye, a bloody tooth. I remember her telling tales about her bruises: she fell, she hit her face on a door. I remember the inability of some people she confided in to believe that she was being abused.

Before Eric, I had never been in an abusive relationship. I had never been with an alcoholic. I had to figure out what to do. It took me a while to make the connection between my mother's experience with domestic violence and my own. Eric didn't hit me outside of the bedroom.

I wasn't dealing with sexual harassment or assault in the workplace. My situation wasn't like that of the women who encountered Russell Simmons or Harvey Weinstein, both of whom had enablers who turned a blind eye until the entire world could see. I entered into it willingly; I walked through the door with Eric. I even felt sorry for him. I thought, "Poor him, he's so depressed, and he's dealing with so much. So many people are putting pressure on him to save the world."

Unlike some of the abusers unmasked by the Me Too movement, Eric was a serial monogamist. He didn't need to abuse dozens or hundreds of women to satisfy his hunger for power. He didn't need a different woman to abuse every day. He had me for almost a year.

Once, during the day, out of nowhere, he said that he was getting bored because he didn't have anything like a three-way to look forward to. He mentioned friends of mine he found cute and suggested that they might be good candidates. At the time, the scandal around the divorce of Mel B of the Spice Girls and her partner had recently broken; her ex had coerced her into having three-ways. I asked, "Do you really want to take that kind of risk?" I knew I wasn't going to have a three-way, just as I knew I wasn't going to have my scars removed or get a boob job, but I was scared to tell him so. Instead, I tried to show him how a three-way would have negative consequences. I thought, "If I can't change how he thinks, maybe I can change how he behaves."

I was putting up with treatment I had never tolerated before in a partner. Perhaps I was fortunate not to have encountered an abuser until Eric. But why was I staying with Eric? I feel there is no real explanation but rather a confluence of many layers. As a child who had witnessed abuse, I could have been more likely to become a victim. As a woman who had been abandoned by her previous partner, I could have been psychologically more vulnerable. I didn't want to be alone, and I didn't want to be abandoned by a partner again. As an organizer who wanted to make the world a better place, I was attracted to Eric's stardom as a progressive advocate. I work hard every day to understand how I got into and stayed in a relationship that was so damaging to my soul. I heard the applause when Eric spoke, and I got swept up in it. Applause can be blinding.

5

DEMEAN

I have sympathy for those who harm me. I always wonder what it is about their history that made them harmful; I want to understand them. But I also know that the older I get, the less I should tolerate those who treat me badly; cumulatively their actions take a toll.

From the home to the school to the street to the workplace, abuse is all around us. The different settings result in most of us dealing, sometimes daily, with micro- and macroaggressions. I think about the insults I've had hurled at me from the time I was a child: the mean girl in elementary school who criticized my black lips; the ex-wife of my former boyfriend, who referred to me as "that Paki"; the old man on a London street who said, "Coolie bugger bastard, go home."

I think about toxic work environments. On a few occasions, I've put up with far more than I should have. When I was in my twenties and started producing films, a fellow producer was constantly second-guessing and berating me. After months and months of taking it and hoping it would go away, I finally said to him, "Fuck you"—which was not my style, but I had had enough and felt I had to shut him up.

Another time, about twenty years later, a colleague—sadly, another woman of color—had it in for me from the moment I walked through the door. She routinely dismissed my ideas and criticized me. She also sought out every opportunity to make me feel that I didn't belong, such as removing me from company event lists. I knew I wasn't alone because other women told me about having had similar experiences with her.

I sent an article by Eileen Hoenigman Meyer to the human resources director at my job because it depicted what I had been enduring with my colleague: "If you find yourself working alongside that colleague who routinely undercuts you in meetings, puts you down in conversations or criticizes your work in front of others, take note. Those are telltale signs that he or she may be threatened by you. It's difficult to exhibit your professional best, while also trying to deflect the shade that your colleague is throwing your way."

Sometimes women target other women because they think there's not enough space for everyone. But I believe in making space. There is enough room. Still, when someone's threatened by you, there's little you can do. After that experience, I vowed never to put up with such treatment again.

Demeaning behavior in the workplace has its own negative psychological repercussions. Such behavior in the home, in a romantic situation, is suffocating. With Eric, I sometimes felt as though he was trying to crush me, if not kill me, with his demeaning behavior. In *Coercive Control: How Men Entrap Women in Personal Life*, Evan Stark wrote, "To make contemporary women their personal property, the modern man must effectively stand against the tide of history, degrading women into a position of subservience that the progress of civilization has made obsolete." More stinging than Eric's slaps was his verbal abuse: that he insisted on calling me his property and his slave during sex, that he criticized my scars and wanted me to get them removed by a plastic surgeon. I was disgusted that he wanted me to call him "Daddy" and referred to me as his daughter when he himself had a daughter. That was why, when he gave me a choice of calling him "Master" or "Daddy," I picked "Master." But that resulted in more of the slave fantasies he inflicted on me.

His attacks on my scars were symbolic of everything horrible he did to me. When I wore V-necks, he would look at my scar and tell me to get rid of it. While on a plane, I saw in the shopping guide a T-shirt that read, "Scars are like tattoos but with better stories." I wear my scars as reminders of what I have been through. They mark me and, in a way, comfort me. Sometimes scars are not visible. Sometimes they come in the form of stories.

When the *New Yorker* story came out, many people doubted that somebody like me could have let such abuse happen. But I have weaknesses. Eric figured out what they were and seized on them. He once said, "Sometimes I look at you, and I'm like, 'Wow.' Sometimes I'm not sure." A comment like that, in isolation, is a jerky thing to say. But taken in the context of the totality of Eric's behavior and actions, it was part of a pattern to demean me and make me feel less than. As Patricia Evans wrote, "Verbal abuse is secretive. . . . [It] becomes more intense over time. The partner becomes used to and adapted to it. . . .

Verbal abuse consistently discounts the partner's perception of the abuse."

For Thanksgiving 2016, Eric wanted to host a "Jew-Bu" celebration at his home for a small group of friends from his meditation circle. He wanted to have the event catered, but he asked me to make a curry to add to the meal. I spent hours buying the ingredients and preparing the dish, but before everyone arrived, he tasted what I had made and said it wasn't good. He didn't want to serve it. I was incredibly hurt. I had been cooking since I was a child, first for my parents and then in various restaurants. In high school, I had worked at a place called Raspberries in Andover, Massachusetts, which would offer "Tanya's Tuesday Special." I liked to make Thai or Indian dishes. In college, I had been a cook at one of the first fine-dining restaurants that catered to a gay clientele in Boston. It was called Club Café, and my friend Thomas had played the piano in the lounge. As an adult, I had hosted dinner parties for which I had made elaborate multicourse meals. But Eric didn't like my cooking. My curry went unserved and was thrown away.

This analysis by Patricia Evans would later resonate with me: "Verbal abuse is, in a sense, built into our culture. One-upmanship, defeating, putting down, topping, countering, manipulating, criticizing, hard selling, and intimidating are accepted as fair games by many. When these power plays are enacted in a relationship and denied by the perpetrator, confusion results." I felt as though I had failed Eric with my cooking, and perhaps that was his intention. As long as he could make me doubt myself, gaslight me, he could control me.

Writing this book sank me into a profound depression. Reviewing all the notes I had taken in real time brought back the experience of being with someone who had made me feel extremely bad about myself. It also triggered memories of how I had felt belittled by important people in my life ever since I was a child.

I do not have good memories of childhood. The friction between my parents made for an unhappy home. I really do believe that my parents tried their best with regard to how they treated me, but they took their frustrations out on me. My father tried to make me feel sorry for him. My mother tried to control me.

I wet the bed a lot as a child. I also sometimes wet myself when awake. I remember standing in my kindergarten class as my mother came to pick me up after a Christmas pageant. She was standing in the doorway and could tell I needed to go to the bathroom. She was nudging me with her eyes to make haste and come to her, but I was frozen in my tracks. As urine streamed down my legs, I felt as though I was in a dark tunnel. I heard the teacher say, "Oh, someone has had an accident."

My mother grabbed my hand and took me away. She was embarrassed; I was sad. When those moments of wetting myself happened, I felt terribly lacking in agency over my body. In elementary school, I was bullied at times. Black girls picked on me, and white girls picked on me, too. There was the mean girl who taunted me about my "black lips"; other kids called me "Tonto" or "Pocahontas." I went along with it. I kept quiet. That was what I usually did: I kept quiet.

In high school, I was the rare girl taking quantum mechanics and vector calculus at the same time. I threw myself into my studies and focused on friends and teachers who helped me thrive. And I had a flair for the avant-garde. I got into acting; theater got me out of my shell, my skin.

That moment after the Christmas pageant when I was four years old and wet myself in front of my whole class is one of my most vivid memories. To this day, I am prone to stage fright. I think I love theater in part because it helps me face my fears.

I was a shy child, made more so by the feeling that I had secrets to hide about my life at home, because I was a witness to horrific domestic violence. I had bouts of not feeling present in this world. There were moments I thought of disappearing. I didn't think of killing myself. I was scared of weapons and blood. But I struggled to find reasons to live. Looking back, I wonder how things might have been different for me as a child if I had seen a therapist, if my mother had seen a therapist, if our whole family had been in counseling. But instead, we concealed our pain.

When I was an adult, as I was cleaning out boxes in my mother's home, I came across a stack of old report cards. Comment after comment from various teachers echoed that fact: I was quiet. One teacher wrote, "Tanya seems shy out of almost excessive respect for everyone." But I was also at the top of my class, and I would rather be smart than loud.

As strong and confident as I seem now, I have my weaknesses, and their roots go back to my childhood.

Eric had told me about his painful childhood. When his parents had divorced, they had had such animus toward each other that they had insisted on calling Eric by two different names; one parent called him by his first name, the other by his middle name. He was essentially always a bifurcated person. I thought it made sense that his favorite television shows, such as *Sneaky Pete* and *The Americans*, were about people who led double lives.

Toward the end of our relationship, when I was mostly staying at my own apartment, I had to go by his place to pick up my Massachusetts General Hospital ID card; I was about to leave for my annual follow-up CT scan. When I walked in, I saw him with more open eyes. Now that I had distance and more objectivity, I saw less of the mask that had kept me with him. I asked how he was doing, meaning on an emotional level, and he prattled on about his poll numbers being down and his fund-raising goals being off. He seemed hollow.

He said he was trying to be mindful of making me feel bad about myself. A few minutes later, he asked if I was wearing perfume. I said yes. He said it was "strong," in a negative way. I had on the same perfume I had always worn, the one he had usually said he loved.

Intimate partner violence tends to happen in the shadows, behind closed doors, cloaked in secrecy. As Evan Stark explained, "Without an 'audience' for their victimization, the 8 to 10 million women experiencing coercive control in the United States remain in a twilight zone, disconnected and undocumented." As I reflect on how I got into an abusive relationship for the first time as a woman in her forties—one who, in the intervening years between childhood and middle age, became an independent person—I think that the little girl in me is still there, feeling bad about herself, and she needs to be set free. Writing it out like this is part of that process.

6

ABUSE

When I was first dealing with cancer, a doctor friend told me that if you scan anyone on the street, you'll probably find something wrong with him or her. Following from that analogy, I believe that if you scratch the surface of most people, you'll probably find a history of abuse.

The pattern of abuse in my relationship with Eric was becoming clearer. Nonetheless, I was having a harder time reconciling my experience of him with the outside world's perception of him. He was not the man I'd thought he was. He was a hypocrite.

But I was still mostly keeping my impression to myself. I would speak in hushed tones with a few trusted friends about his drinking and controlling behavior, about his not letting me eat chicken. But I was frightened to tell anyone about his abuse in the sexual context. On the one hand, I felt embarrassed and ashamed. On the other hand, I felt protective of him. If I told anyone details about the abuse, I wouldn't be able to take it back. And what if he did change for the better? Couldn't he change if he wanted to?

My heart and mind were not working with clarity. I was persuading myself that the situation would turn around if I stuck with it. I ask myself sometimes, "How could I have been so stupid?"

But after I shared my story, so many friends told me about their own experiences. It was comforting to feel that I wasn't alone, but it was also disheartening to be aware of so many painful stories. One friend talked about a relationship that had been verbally and financially abusive. She said, "He slapped me once, and I broke up with him. So in some ways, the intimate partner violence was what liberated me. I wondered why I hadn't left earlier and began to question what my own role was—not in the sense of 'blaming the victim,' but every relationship is an ecosystem, and I no longer wanted to be part of any ecosystem like that!"

Another friend described a relationship she had rekindled with a longtime lover. During one encounter, she had noticed he was acting strange and distant but hadn't realized he was using a variety of drugs. That night, when she was half asleep, "he stormed through the bedroom door and forced himself on me without speaking or consent. I didn't even seem to exist as a person in that moment. He was hurting me. Was he raping me? I remember thinking 'He doesn't see me as a human being. There is no one on this earth who cares about me.'" They broke up that week.

Our collective storytelling felt like a bloodletting. I saw more clearly how capable, independent women become ensnared. Even fierce women get abused.

Elizabeth Méndez Berry is a former journalist who wrote several pieces about domestic violence in the music industry, one of which, "Love Hurts," won an ASCAP Foundation Deems Taylor/Virgil Thomson Award for music journalism. She told me, "Once you get to the point of physical abuse, there's usually so much emotional scaffolding that breaks you down. At the point that he hits you for the first time, he's often built up to that with lots of corrosive behavior."

In my relationship, I knew that I was being increasingly mentally and physically tormented. We couldn't have sex without his beating me, trying to strangle me, or insisting that I call him "Master" or "Daddy" and submit to serving as his property. I want to be clear that I believe desire is subjective; what's scary for one person can be kinky for another. But in my case, all that wasn't consensual; it wasn't exciting; it wasn't S and M; it wasn't sexual playacting; it was abusive, demeaning, threatening behavior. I felt like Offred in *The Handmaid's Tale*, who described sex with the Commander in this way: "What's going on in this room . . . is not exciting. It has nothing to do with passion or love or romance or any of those other notions we used to titillate ourselves with. It has nothing to do with sexual desire, at least for me. . . . Arousal and orgasm are no longer thought necessary."

Eric was taking out his need for power and his anxiety on me. It happened at night, in the dark, when I was naked, when it was more difficult to make an assertive decision. It happened when we were most intimate and I was most vulnerable, sometimes half asleep in bed. When I told him that I was in pain or asked him to stop, he ignored and belittled me. It felt like a bad dream.

In the morning, I would wake up, and another day would begin when I would see his good side, and I would be hopeful. Also, we didn't have sex every day. He told me he was old. The less I had sex with him, the more I could avoid his abuse in the bedroom. Often, I deliberately tried to go to bed early.

As time went by, the slaps during sex got harder and the emotional and verbal abuse more frequent. I began to feel I was in hell. But he was also charming and charismatic, often supportive. I was constantly being pushed away from and pulled toward him.

I thought I was mentally and emotionally stronger than him; I didn't realize that he was breaking me down. My former husband had left me when I was down, and I believe I was in an emotionally delicate state after the dissolution of my marriage. Also, the physical abuse that my mother had experienced from my father and that I had witnessed made me more vulnerable to abuse myself.

When I saw my father hit my mother, it was in our living room, in our kitchen, not in their bed. As a result, I dissociated what I was experiencing with Eric from what I had witnessed as a child. If he had hit me in the living room or kitchen, I think I would have been out of there almost immediately. I had always thought of myself as someone who would say, "The moment a man hits you, walk away. Walk away and don't come back unless he says he is getting professional help."

But the kind of violence I experienced during sex with Eric was hard to talk about. And I was more afraid to leave him than to stay with him and deal with his abuse. I always had it in the back of my mind that Eric could inflict great harm on me. He had, after all, said that if we broke up, he would have to kill me. Would he snap if we did break up?

I have friends who dated powerful men and were similarly threatened. In some cases, the men tried to realize their threats, hiring private investigators to track the women's movements and talking about hitmen. My friends lived in mortal fear of those men, and to this day they suffer from post-traumatic stress disorder (PTSD). I understand now what PTSD feels like. It's hard to describe, but David J. Morris, in his book *The Evil Hours: A Biography of Post-Traumatic Stress Disorder*, explained it as "essentially a junk drawer of disconnected symptoms, which include a numbing of the emotions, hypervigilance (always being 'amped up'), social isolation, and a variety of intrusive manifestations, such as nightmares and hallucinations."

I wanted Eric to get help and for us to work things out. I thought the abuse could end. I thought, as do so many women of all types who are in such a situation, that he could change. Yet, unless an abuser is willing to acknowledge the abuse and dig deep and do the work, he won't change.

It's not as if he didn't know he had a problem.

One night in the spring of 2017, he told me, "A friend called and said she heard that I had a reputation for being rough with women."

We were in the dining room, he on one side of the long table and I on the other.

I kept silent. I didn't respond. I thought the friend was right and wondered if she knew exactly how rough he was. I filed the remark away in my mind.

Later, through Jane Mayer and Ronan Farrow's investigation,

I would discover that in fact I was one in a long line of women who had experienced abuse by Eric and that he seemed to customize the abuse, in a perhaps intuitive or feral way, with each woman. He and I didn't have a volatile relationship; we didn't have arguments. With other women, apparently, he had. He had fought with them and hit them outside the bedroom. But the constant in each of his relationships was the need to hit women and dehumanize them.

Eric engaged in a pattern of abuse, and there was nothing ambiguous about it. I know I didn't trigger his sexual sadism; he had been like that before I walked through the door. But he conditioned me to accept his treatment.

Eric's violent behavior in the bedroom continued to be reinforced by his frequent criticism of me, of the way I looked, my weight, what I wore, my hair. I couldn't even sit at a table and work without hearing about it. I kept trying to modulate myself, to be more conscientious about my appearance and my habits. But as Patricia Evans explained, the partner of an abuser must realize "that there is no 'way she can be' to prevent the abuser from venting his anger on her. Speaking more gently, listening more attentively, being more supportive, more interesting, more learned, more fun, thinner, cuter, or classier—being more anything will not work."

In my situation, the abuse was compounded by Eric's addiction to alcohol and prescription drugs. Those substances impaired his ability to function coherently and fueled his violence. And I was the person closest to him, standing by to witness the bifurcation.

A man can't profess to be a champion of women politically and crush them privately. Eric was creating his own undoing. It was as if he were saying "Catch me! Here I am." He was laying the groundwork for the unearthing of his abuse by being so visible as an advocate for women.

It's mind-boggling that Eric could pass laws to help women in the abstract while harming real women in his own life. His advocacy was a form of atonement but also of deflection. It was as if he were declaring "I can't be guilty of these private crimes because of what I do publicly."

Of course, this affliction of many men, to inflict harm on women, transcends political lines. When people have money or power or both, they can have impunity. They can be entitled. They don't have to do the right thing.

Where did that behavior come from? What was it in Eric's upbringing and experience that made him do it? I believe it came partially from his deep animus toward his mother. Eric often talked about his mother having been crazy and controlling, and he took out his pent-up hatred for her on me and other girlfriends. It is a sad, sad tale from start to finish. But being victimized as a child doesn't give anyone the right to abuse women. Eric knew he was bad, but he didn't actually want to or have the courage to confront his abusive behavior.

I thought I could understand him: the external control versus the internal torment, the tension between how one seems and how one feels. I know what it's like to want to disappear but be unable to, to want to destroy yourself as much as you can so long as you can still stand and work and speak. Eric tried to counter his addictions with meditation. But he was turning to the spiritual world with the hope that it would take away his pain without actually dealing with the pain itself.

While I was deciding whether to come forward, I watched

the documentary *One of Us*, by Heidi Ewing and Rachel Grady, about the pain inflicted on people in the Hasidic community who choose to leave it. One subject, Etty, described how her husband had abused her physically and verbally, yet the local courts had taken their kids away from her when she had divorced him. Her husband had been shielded by their religious community. Her story highlighted the fact that when women in custody battles make allegations of abuse, the judges may punish them for making the allegations. It's almost as if the women are being told, "How dare you?" This movie had a profound impact on me. It helped me decide to speak out.

The day after my story became public, Megan McArdle, a columnist for the *Washington Post*, wrote an op-ed in response. My story had triggered her to recall being hit by a boyfriend twenty-five years before. She wrote about how hard it had been to come forward and how hard it had been to reconcile the person who had hit her with the man she loved: "You're picturing a rage-filled monster, an archetype: 'the abuser.' I'm remembering the man, who was funny and brilliant. And who was, like Schneiderman, a staunch public feminist. There were many reasons I wanted to be with him, and none of them were simple, because neither was he." Her op-ed was titled "I Went Back to a Man Who Hit Me. I'm Still Thinking About Why." I was grateful to McArdle for her words, which resonated with the conflict I felt with regard to Eric, his good side and his dark side.

It turned out that a number of my friends had thought that something was wrong in my relationship but had refrained from asking. If they had asked, I might have told them it was a fairy tale that had become a nightmare.

THE NIGHTMARE

When I was a child, I often remembered and recorded my dreams. They typically were (and continue to be) coherent narratives. Sometimes I would tell my mother about a dream, and she would shush me and say, "What nonsense." But I have always believed that dreams will tell me things if I let them. I had a dream a few months before my father died of lung cancer that my mother and I were on vacation while he lay curled up on the floor back at home. In the dream, my mother got a call from someone saying, "Dead." And my mother cried, "Daddy has died! Daddy's died! And we're not there!"

Soon after having the dream, I booked a ticket to visit my family in Los Angeles and spend more time with my father. I was with him in the hospital when he died. One of the most striking memories I carry to this day is of looking into his eyes as he took his last breath. His body deflated like a balloon. I can see his expression now in my mind. He seemed so far away.

When I was a child, I loved going to horror movies. My

father took me to basically anything I wanted to see: *The Amityville Horror, Friday the 13th*. He was intrigued by my fascination with those kinds of films. He'd say, "Tanya, you're so macabre."

I enjoyed putting my hands over my eyes when the scenes got especially scary. I enjoyed jumping in my seat, the adrenaline rush. But then, afterward, at home, I would have to sleep with a light on, scared of the monsters I imagined were hiding under my bed. The nightmares felt very real.

In *The Gift of Fear: And Other Survival Signals That Protect Us from Violence*, Gavin de Becker wrote about the difference between good fear and bad fear. The latter prevents us from living our best life. The former heightens our sensitivity to people, places, and things we should avoid; one might call it intuition. He explained that "when it comes to danger, intuition is always right in at least two important ways: (1) It is always in response to something. (2) It always has your best interest at heart."

By the spring of 2017, I was making more and more plans to go away. When I wasn't around Eric and in his environment, there was more mental space for my intuition about him to kick in, and it was supported by my dreams.

In one of them, I was in an office with my literary agent. A woman in a suit stopped at the door and said she had heard we were speaking with a reporter about the attorney general. What could we tell her about that? We played dumb. After she left, I realized I was in danger. I told my agent to be very careful about whom she told anything to. I decided I had to pack up everything in the office, including all my clothes, and leave no trace. But I struggled to figure out where I should take everything. Where would everything be safe? I knew that I couldn't take it back to my apartment in Manhattan. There was too much risk of someone breaking in. I was especially concerned about my hard drive and computer. The dream continued with my preparing to leave the office and realizing that I was at One World Trade Center, where I was working at *Glamour*. Then the moment I was dreading arrived: Eric himself approached and asked what was going on. I pretended that nothing was happening. I tried to deflect attention from how much I had told the reporter.

I woke up. The nightmares were starting to drain me.

When I went to my twenty-five-year college reunion, I felt freer and happier than I had in months. I stayed in a freshman dorm and, with my classmates, hosted all-night parties there. Many people had come with their partners and families. I was alone, but word had spread about who my boyfriend was.

One friend said, "I hear you're dating a very important person."

I smiled. Inside, I thought, "If only you knew how miserable I am."

When I returned from the reunion, Eric continued to complain about how I took up too much space. I told him I could stay at my place. The nights I spent downtown made me realize how sleep deprived I was, how cut off from my friends and support network I had been.

For the month of July, I went to a family wedding in Sri Lanka and then to Portland to work on a show. While I was away, when I spoke with Eric on the phone, he was always kind and calm. He said he was working on himself. He was planning to go to a meditation retreat upstate. I was hopeful that when I returned, things would be different. I missed the way he had been toward me early in our relationship. I longed for that person, who had seemed too good to be true, to come back.

The morning I arrived in New York City, I had a shoot with Samantha Bee for *Glamour*. I mentioned Eric to her, that he was my boyfriend, and we talked about the possibility of having him on her show. That night, I met Eric for dinner. He said that he was still working on himself and that he wanted space. I was actually hurt—I really did have hope that after a month apart, the peace he was feeling and the self-analysis he had engaged in while I was in Portland would have made a difference. A few weeks later, he went to another meditation retreat, and we had dinner after he returned. We were at Gabriel's, where we had had one of our first dates, across from Jazz at Lincoln Center. He said he was still working on himself and wanted space. At the end of the meal, I said I was going to stay at my place. He was angry that I didn't want to come home with him. Even though he had said he wanted space, he became visibly upset. He seemed like a little boy who wasn't getting his way. I felt yet again that he was treating me like a yo-yo, pushing me away and then pulling me back.

I wasn't ready to break up, but I could sense myself beginning to detach. I was focusing more on what was best for me. Still, I kept hoping that Eric was the man he claimed to be: a champion of women, a protector of our rights. But that wasn't the case. He had me in a committed relationship for almost a year. All the while, I was trying to find sense where there was none. And as we know now in painful detail, he was one of legions of powerful predatory men.

The list is endless. The perpetrators are of different ages, colors, professions, and political leanings. Their memories of the events are different from the victims', but their saying the victims' stories aren't true doesn't mean we can give them the benefit of the doubt.

Some of the men I had met—Weinstein on multiple occasions. During the 2017 Tribeca Film Festival, I went with Eric to a twenty-fifth-anniversary screening party for *Reservoir Dogs*. Weinstein was thrilled that such a big-shot New York State politician had taken the time to come to a party in Brooklyn. Much of the original cast was there. Ron Burkle, Weinstein's close pal and an investor in the Weinstein Company, was also there. While Eric said hi to him, I slipped away. I had heard that Burkle was an intimate terrorist whose victims were too mortally scared for their own safety to come forward. I had also heard that he was formerly pals with Bill Clinton and Jeffrey Epstein and that they would hang out together on Burkle's private plane, which was referred to as Air Fuck One.

Another time I met Weinstein was at Planned Parenthood's hundredth-anniversary gala. Eric and I were whisked to an elevated greenroom. Hillary Clinton was there, and she referred to Weinstein as an "old friend." He took Eric aside. He was sweating profusely and started rambling about amfAR, the AIDS charity.

"They're going to skewer me," he said to Eric. I inferred that he was referring to the press, though I didn't know what he was afraid of being skewered for.

Eric tried to calm him down and said his office would follow up with Weinstein's office to see how it could help. I think Eric enjoyed being the guy that people in power had to come to because he had authority over their businesses and charities.

Months later, on September 23, 2017, Megan Twohey wrote

in the *New York Times* about how Weinstein was being investigated for pretending to raise millions for the charity while
scheming to have the money returned to a theater project of his
own. Within two weeks of the article appearing, she and Jodi
Kantor would break the story of Weinstein's abuse of women.
Vanity Fair's subsequent piece about the amfAR scandal was
titled "'Nothing About This Deal Feels Right to Me': Inside
Harvey Weinstein's Other Nightmare."

Another perpetrator I met—at a benefit, through a mutual
friend—was Louis C.K. I remember he complimented my
dress, a black-and-gold caftan, and he was perfectly nice. But
he and other perpetrators are bifurcated individuals. They are
narcissists with money who get off on sexually intimidating
and overpowering women. And they typically have a fleet of
enablers: executives, producers, agents, a whole system designed to conceal their crimes. The enablers usually wait until
the perpetrators they supported go all the way down before
jumping ship.

When Ivanka Trump was asked on *CBS This Morning*
whether she had been complicit in her father's misdeeds, she
deflected the question. She seemed not to understand the
meaning of the word. Thereafter, internet searches for "complicit" spiked by 11,000 percent. Women who support perpetrators are both complicit and psychologically warped. Those
who stay in relationships with abusive men often do so because
they are financially dependent, because they have kids and
don't want to break up the family, because they don't think they
will have an identity on their own, or because they enjoy the
status of being the partner of a powerful man. Before I dated
Eric, I had been someone who would ask, even about my own

mother, "Why isn't she standing up? Why isn't she speaking out? Why isn't she running away?" And then it happened to me, and I got it.

When I started telling people, out of self-preservation, about my abusive experiences with Eric, I was still scared what he might do if I left him. But I finally had people responding that what had happened was not okay, that I needed to run.

A close friend called to check in. We have a telepathic ability to know when to reach out to each other. I told her that things were strange with Eric and that I was figuring out what to do. She started asking questions that elicited details from me. She asked if he hit me. I said yes, in the bedroom during sex. I could feel her growing more concerned. She asked if I would be willing to speak with her friend who was a domestic violence expert and lawyer, Jennifer Friedman. I said yes, and my friend connected us by email. Friedman and I set up a time for a call. As I described my experience to her, I was disgusted by the words coming out of my mouth, the awareness that I had put up with his mistreatment. But it took my confiding in her for me to see that Eric was never going to change and that he had probably done the same thing to other women.

I finally told my therapist, Dr. Mark Epstein, about the abuse. Before then, I had been telling him about Eric's drinking and his controlling behavior, about how I was feeling sleep deprived. He had encouraged me to spend more time away from Eric. As soon as I told him about the physical abuse (around the time I had spoken with Friedman), he said I had to get out.

During that session with Mark, I asked him, "What do you really think about all this?"

He said, "He's a pig." He also said that he was sad for me

because he had been excited about the relationship. He felt bad that he hadn't been able to help me earlier.

I said, "Well, I told you about the drinking, controlling, criticism, and sleep deprivation, but I didn't tell you for almost a year about everything else that was happening."

He said, "And that's an important part of the story. I have patients who wait seven years to tell me about their sexual abuse as a child."

Until then, I had been scared to tell anyone because I had known the situation was wrong and because I had thought Eric would get better.

In my case, I also felt that if I talked about the physical abuse, it would become real. In *No Visible Bruises: What We Don't Know About Domestic Violence Can Kill Us*, Rachel Louise Snyder wrote, "[Physical abuse] is most often hidden from even one's closest confidantes, and on many occasions the physical violence is far less damaging than the emotional and verbal violence."

I had tried to deal with Eric directly to turn things around. When I talked with him about the physical and sexual violence, he made it seem like a game, even though I told him it didn't feel good and I didn't like it. When I talked with him about the verbal and psychological abuse, he said he was aware of it but had excuses: he was depressed; times were turbulent; he was going to get help; he was going to work on himself. I would cling to the hope that he was telling the truth, but as Patricia Evans explained, "This first stage of recognition is the beginning of the partner's change from doubting herself to doubting her mate."

I'd lived through nightmares before. When my former husband had left me, I'd felt abandoned. I hadn't known which way was up. The intensity of his cruelty, especially so soon after my surgeries, had hurt me severely. He had agreed to go to a couples counselor. After the first session, the counselor had asked me, cautiously, "Tanya, do you think there's someone else?" At the time, I hadn't known for sure, though I had suspected. And of course, it was later confirmed that he had indeed been with someone else.

The situation with my ex-husband felt like boilerplate romantic trouble compared to the nightmare I was engulfed in with Eric. The panic attacks, the heart palpitations, the spontaneous shaking—they are all terrifying. And his position of legal and political power only heightened my fear. He was a New York State politician with a big national profile who was increasingly seen as a savior of democracy. Moreover, if the president of the United States was not being held accountable as a perpetrator of sexual violence, how could I expect Eric to be?

In 2018, the W. M. Keck Center for Collaborative Neuroscience at Rutgers University released a study about stressful life memories related to ruminative thoughts in women with a history of sexual violence. In the piece, published in *Frontiers in Psychiatry*, coauthors Emma Millon, Han Yan Chang, and Tracey Shors wrote, "More than one in every four women in the world experience sexual violence (SV) in their lifetime, most often as teenagers and young adults. These traumatic experiences leave memories in the brain, which are difficult if not impossible to forget."

Subsequently, Jessica Ravitz and Arman Azad explained in an article for CNN, "Memories That Last: What Sexual Assault Survivors Remember and Why," "Victims of sexual violence reported 44% more depressive symptoms and twice as many symptoms of anxiety than those who had no history with sexual violence." As the Keck Center study showed, women who've experienced a sexual assault are more likely to remember their assault than other sorts of trauma, such as car accidents.

It took me a while to open up to friends and experts and to realize that I needed to figure out how to get out. I worried that those around Eric would have his back if I made accusations against him. I needed to protect myself.

I thought, "I'm brave, but I'm also fragile."

After I connected with Jennifer Friedman, I had more of the tools I needed to extricate myself from my relationship with Eric as gently as possible without setting him off. With her help, I made a plan.

8

WHAT IS INTIMATE VIOLENCE?

Until I experienced intimate partner violence (IPV), I didn't understand what it was. Even after I started going through it, it took me a while to name it. I had a hard time opening up to friends, but when I did—and especially after my story became public—there was an outpouring of support from friends and even strangers, many of whom shared their own experiences. Once someone shares her own story, the floodgates open.

When I asked Rachna Khare, the executive director of Daya Houston, an organization for South Asian victims of abuse, for her definition of the issue, she responded, "Intimate partner violence is a pattern of abusive behavior used to maintain power and control over a partner. The abuse can be physical, emotional, verbal, sexual, or financial—to name a few. Intimate partner violence can occur in any kind of intimate relationship."

"Intimate violence" is a subset of domestic and intimate partner violence. It happens during sex and is entwined with other patterns of abuse. What makes intimate violence so insidious is that the victim might not immediately realize it's wrong. The abuser can manipulate the victim into thinking his or her behavior in the bedroom is acceptable, or the abuser can break down the victim to withstand being harmed in the bedroom.

Domestic violence is the number one reason for calls to 9-1-1. However, while victims want to be free from violence, they might hesitate to seek help from the police in order to avoid getting caught up in the criminal justice system, which is especially fraught for people of color. The movement to defund the police pressures state and city governments to redirect support to grassroots, community-specific organizations. Those organizations should include domestic violence organizations and shelters so that they can more effectively provide services, such as restorative justice programs, to victims.

According to the Centers for Disease Control and Prevention, "About 1 in 4 women and nearly 1 in 10 men have experienced contact sexual violence, physical violence, and/or stalking by an intimate partner during their lifetime and reported some form of IPV-related impact." Furthermore, about 11 million women and 5 million men who reported experiencing such violence first did so before the age of eighteen. Although intimate violence affects both women and men in both opposite-sex and same-sex relationships, the vast majority of violence—rape, murder, assault—is committed by men.

Before I met Eric, I often considered what I would do if I were attacked by a man. I had envisioned situations in which I might be ambushed, either in the woods near my place in Portland, Oregon, or walking down a dark street to my apartment in New York City. I imagined that I would start screaming like a banshee, kick the guy in the balls, yell at the top of my lungs, and flail my arms around as if I were possessed.

But here I was acquiescing to abuse in the home, at the hands of someone I knew.

A World Health Organization report on intimate partner violence outlined some of the reasons why women don't leave violent relationships: fear of retaliation, lack of alternative means of economic support, and concern for their children. Community and societal factors, such as norms that link manhood with dominance and aggression, also play a part.

Women are blamed for staying and blamed for fighting back. They're blamed for getting into the relationship in the first place. That happened to me—a friend said I should really think about what it was about me that had allowed me to get involved with Eric. It wasn't helpful for her to say that, but I forgave her for it. I also thought, "His behavior had been going on for a very long time. I helped stop it."

Before my story of intimate violence became public, I had been known for my work, my advocacy, and my art. When I had written *The Big Lie*, about my fertility struggles, I had been largely in control of the narrative. But here, the story and my character were being spun by outlet after outlet in a way over which I had no control.

Something else happened as well. As I opened up to friends, ones I'd known for years, they told me for the first time details of their own experiences of being abused: one whose boyfriend had broken her rib, another whose ex-husband would push her hard against a wall in front of their children. A young director in her twenties whom I was mentoring told me about a housemate who had gotten drunk and assaulted her.

One friend had been dependent on her husband to drive her. She knew how to drive, but he had made sure that she didn't get a chance to do it. They'd had only one car and lived in a town where there was no other way to get around. The physical abuse had usually happened in the car, when he literally had control of the keys. After she had gotten him arrested during an especially violent fight, he had told her from jail that he'd given her address and phone number to fellow inmates who were murderers and soon to be released. She began to sleep with a butcher knife under her bed. She and I were having dinner at a restaurant when she told me the story. I couldn't believe that the strong, positive woman across from me had endured such horror and fear.

The stories of my friends involved varying degrees of violence, but what united them was the trauma inflicted, the violence not reciprocated, the fear, the self-blame. Many people would rather that women suffer than speak their truths. But we need to talk about these things because as long as we don't, the perpetrators can and will get away with them. Just because they're not doing those things the majority of the time doesn't mean we have to tolerate their actions. Just because they may have performed some good deeds doesn't mean they get a pass. They have to be called out.

I remember numerous times I was able to evade threatening sexual situations with a man. Once when I was walking near my high school, a man in a light blue suit standing in the bushes pulled down his pants and exposed himself to me. When I was in my twenties, a director insisted on seeing me naked before casting me. When I was in my thirties, at a bar, a famous married actor said nonchalantly that he wanted me to come to his hotel and sit on his face. After I didn't, I heard, he got into a fight with a hotel concierge.

After the Me Too movement took off post Weinstein, there was a relentless stream of stories about a predator or a predatory system. It was easy to get caught up in the horror of each revelation. We might have thought it didn't bother us until we heard another person's story, and then we were triggered. But the triggering was also a releasing. It was a releasing of our own trauma as well as generational trauma. In my case, it was the trauma passed down from my mother's abuse at the hands of my father. It was also the trauma of the murder of my paternal grandmother when I was just shy of nine years old. We received the news by telephone. My mother's mother called from Sri Lanka. At first, she said that my paternal grandmother— whom I called Archi—had fallen on her head and died quickly. No suffering. That same day, it came out that she had been ambushed by a large group of men in her home late at night.

Not a thing in the house was touched—not the jewelry, not the statues of Jesus, Mary, Joseph, and St. Bernadette that stood on a ledge on the wall. But they chopped off Archi's nose, slit her throat, beat her, then vanished. On the window were metal bars that Archi had reluctantly just had installed. Those bars had been to protect her. The men had come through the front door.

I remember trying to bring up Archi's death to a relative in Sri Lanka when I was an adult. She put her head down and said, "Don't talk about such things." We have been conditioned to be quiet and not talk about our horrible memories. But we have to share our stories of violence to begin to heal and also to shape the public discourse.

*   *   *

In February 2018, I attended a conversation hosted by PEN America about the Me Too movement. The panelists talked about how some of those denounced were their friends and colleagues. However, taking a utilitarian approach, some suggested that if thousands of women were saved by the outing of serious perpetrators, it might not matter if a few innocent men were unfairly taken down.

That struck me as dangerous thinking. Accusations can happen fast and in a sweeping way, and we should avoid witch hunts. Due process is vital to fairness. I believe in fact-checking allegations. With regard to my experience with Eric, I submitted myself to multiple investigations, first for the *New Yorker* story by Jane Mayer and Ronan Farrow and then for the special prosecutor and other legal entities assigned to examine this case. I knew I had to support the process; I had to be scrutinized. If we don't establish the veracity of allegations and the credibility of the accuser, if we don't distinguish between men behaving badly and men committing horrific acts against women that cause lifelong trauma, we do the Me Too movement a great disservice.

Abusers such as PBS talk show host and coanchor of *CBS This Morning* Charlie Rose and WNYC radio show host John Hockenberry thrived for decades despite many people knowing about their depravity. In the case of Hockenberry, Laura Walker, then the president and CEO of New York Public Radio, enabled him while dismissing complaints from multiple cohosts, who were women of color, about his harassment of them. How can we make victims feel that they will be protected and it is safe to come forward? We have to dismantle thousands of years of patriarchy. That might take thousands more years to achieve, but we can take measures now through education, legislation, and public awareness.

At the PEN panel, the writer Masha Gessen suggested that it might be better to have less sex than one bad sexual encounter. But, she asserted, we should end the conversation with the feeling that we should have more, not less, sex. I myself am not advocating for sexual puritanism. The spectrum of desire is broad and should allow for a variety of experiences. My intent is not to stifle experimentation; it is to prevent harm and trauma, and take misogyny out of the bedroom. That involves communication. It involves questions and cues. It involves mutual respect.

Eric was so skilled at abusing me that I thought I was responsible for it, that something about me had brought it on. Ultimately, I discovered not only that his abuse was *not* specific to me but also that I was part of a pattern that had gone on for years and years. In addition to the women whose accounts were depicted in the *New Yorker*, there were a number of women who reached out to the publication and to me after the story came out. They wanted to talk about their own traumatic experiences with him.

Jess McIntosh, a Democratic strategist, published her own account about Eric. I knew McIntosh but became aware of her experience with him only when I read about it on Elle.com. While she had been a researcher on his state senator campaign, thirteen years before, he had turned a meeting into a date. Even though she had kept saying she had a boyfriend, he kept making moves on her. She was twenty-three; he was fifty. After some making out, she had abruptly gotten out of the car, breaking a string of her grandmother's pearls. In the piece, she wrote, "The truth is that story doesn't have a damn thing to do with me, and maybe that's the worst part. Sometimes we're just at the mercy of the men who decide what's next for us: whether we get hit that night, whether we get home."

Shortly before my story came out, I was with a group of friends who were helping me prepare for tough questions that might come my way from reporters. They asked me to describe explicitly the violence in the bedroom. By that point, I had recounted my experience so many times that I was exhausted, but I spoke clearly. One friend there had recently broken up with her boyfriend, partially because he was an addict. Later that day, she called and said, "You could have been describing what happened to me."

Abuse permeates all aspects of society, and it often begins at home. With the Me Too and Time's Up movements, the focus has not been enough on serial domestic violence. But home is where such behaviors become conditioned, and until we address that root cause, we will never do away with violence in the workplace, violence outside the home; we will never do away with war.

With the advent of the coronavirus pandemic in late 2019/ early 2020, domestic violence was in the news more than I had ever witnessed before. The United Nations Population Fund (UNFPA) estimated that there had been a 20 percent increase globally and that "every three months of lockdown could result in 15 million more cases of domestic abuse than would normally be expected." The most dangerous place in the world for a woman is her own home. Being quarantined with an abusive partner poses greater risks. Victims ordinarily wait to be by themselves before they seek help. They wait for their abuser to go to work. They secretly reach out to friends. They look for openings when they don't have child care obligations. All those options closed down.

Children who were unable to attend school or day care were also at greater risk. My heart broke when I thought of the children who no longer had the opportunity to avoid seeing the violence at home or who might be victims of the violence themselves. I wanted to do something that could help, so I wrote an essay for the *New York Times* entitled "Where Can Domestic Violence Victims Turn During COVID-19?" It ran on March 23, shortly following the shelter-in-place order in New York and many other US states. Among the takeaways from my piece were that self-isolation could lead to a decrease in the ability of victims to seek immediate safety assistance and that friends and loved ones could be a lifeline to those victims; in addition, a rise in domestic violence would happen in the United States, as had already occurred in other countries.

Early in the global pandemic in China, domestic violence reports nearly doubled. The hashtag #AntiDomesticViolence DuringEpidemic trended on the Chinese social media platform Sina Weibo. Eventually lockdowns would take place in other parts of the world, and similar spikes emerged. Spain reported an 18 percent increase in domestic violence calls over in the same period the year before. In France, the police reported an increase of about 30 percent in domestic violence incidences. Those governments tried to combat the crisis by instituting code words at pharmacies and turning hotels into shelters. Canada announced that as part of its COVID-19 Economic Response Plan, it would contribute up to $40 million to shelters and sexual assault centers, with $10 million of these funds dedicated to Indigenous shelters.

On the side of government inaction, Mexico took no steps to address the rise in domestic abuse, even though almost a thousand women had been murdered in the first three months of 2020, an 8 percent spike from the same time last year. Russia, which had decriminalized domestic violence in 2017, continued stalling a bill to recriminalize it. The speaker of Russia's upper-house Federation Council, Valentina Matviyenko, said, "I don't think there will be a surge in domestic violence since families are going through this difficult time together." She was dead wrong; regions around Russia reported increases as high as threefold in calls to hotlines.

During my research for the *New York Times* piece, I spoke with Katie Ray-Jones, the chief executive officer of the National Domestic Violence Hotline. She talked about how an abusive partner could leverage COVID-19 to create fear, isolation, and manipulation. One caller to the Hotline spoke about her husband forcing her to wash her hands repeatedly until they were raw and bleeding. Another partner had threatened to kick a woman out of the house to increase her exposure to the virus. Ray-Jones told me that there had actually been fewer calls in the early days of the lockdown. That was not because domestic violence was happening less but because it was harder for victims to report it. Her biggest worry was that they couldn't reach out for help; they were unable to have a phone conversation when the perpetrator was beside them, and abusers often monitor the phones of their victims.

Meanwhile, cities around the country, such as Seattle, Washington, and San Antonio, Texas, were reporting increases of more than 20 percent in domestic violence calls. Sales of firearms were rising at alarming rates, with about 2 million guns sold in March—"The second-busiest month ever for gun sales, trailing only January 2013, just after President Barack Obama's reelection and the mass shooting at Sandy Hook Elementary School." Perpetrators of gun violence are often perpetrators of domestic violence. The context of the crisis—with the loss of life and economic stability—was exacerbating the stressors that contribute to domestic abuse. I realized that the horror stories will likely become better known after the pandemic ends.

Gloria Steinem, in a conversation with Diane von Furstenberg uploaded to YouTube on May 20, 2020, said in reference to increases in domestic violence, "We're never going to have a democratic peaceful society until we have democratic peaceful homes. . . . We haven't enough addressed the basic problem, which is that men [live in a society which tells them they] have to dominate in order to be masculine."

I have often wondered about how terrifying it would be for men if women could fight back, if they could protect themselves and one another with their bodies alone. Naomi Alderman imagined such a world in her 2016 novel *The Power*: after discovering their hidden physical abilities, women take over in various countries around the world where they were previously enslaved and oppressed, from Saudi Arabia to India to, yes, the United States.

In 2018, a Thomson Reuters survey placed the United States as the tenth most dangerous place in the world for women, the only Western country on the list. (India was number one.) This ranking of the United States stretches across all aspects of the American canvas. The equality and safety of all American women cannot be achieved while that fact holds.

Where do we go from here? We have to chip away at the power of the patriarchy. We have to chip away at the conditioning and behavior that give rise to the devastating statistics. Intimate partner violence has been linked to a wide range of negative health outcomes, including depression, post-traumatic stress and other anxiety disorders, sleep difficulties, eating disorders, and suicide attempts.

It has also been linked to enormous economic setbacks. According to a 2018 study published in the *American Journal of Preventive Medicine*, "the lifetime economic cost associated with medical services for IPV-related injuries, lost productivity from paid work, criminal justice, and other costs was $3.6 trillion. The cost of IPV over a victim's lifetime was $103,767 for women and $23,414 for men." As Rachel Louise Snyder explained in *No Visible Bruises*, "the United States spends as much as twenty-five times more on researching cancer or heart disease than it does on violence prevention, despite the enormous costs of violence to our communities."

The demographics of both abusers and victims cut across racial, economic, and religious lines. However, this cannot be, as Kimberlé Crenshaw, who coined the term "intersectionality," has stated, a "rhetorical strategy" to "exclude or ignore the needs of poor and colored women." The impact of intimate violence—as with so many afflictions in our society, which we witnessed more acutely during the pandemic—disproportionately affects women of color. African Americans make up about 13 percent of the general population, but they make up about 40 percent of the homeless population. The majority of homeless women are survivors of domestic violence. African American and Hispanic women are more likely to be incarcerated than are white women. The majority of incarcerated women are survivors of domestic violence. These facts are not a coincidence.

Seeking help in general and especially during the pandemic could be hard for women of color. In an article by Ashley Southall for the *New York Times*, Margarita Guzmán, the executive director of the Violence Intervention Program, which serves primarily Latin communities, talked about a woman who "wanted to leave her abusive husband, but she decided the risk of exposing herself or her infant to the virus at a shelter was too high."

Calling the police on an abuser—the widely recommended advice for a woman in imminent danger—can be an extremely difficult step for women of color to take. As Crenshaw explained, "Women of color are often reluctant to call the police, a hesitancy likely due to a general unwillingness among people of color to subject their private lives to the scrutiny and control of a police force that is frequently hostile." Black Lives Matter and then the racism reckoning that dovetailed with the pandemic amplified the urgent need to center the experiences of women of color, including trans women who are disproportionately affected by violence, prejudice, and hate. Gender justice is an essential component of racial justice.

The data on women of color and violence are devastating with regard to American Indian and Alaska Native women. According to a 2016 study by the National Institute of Justice, 55.5 percent have experienced physical violence by an intimate partner, higher than any other demographic group. When I watched "An Indigenous Response to #MeToo," a filmed conversation for *Rematriation Magazine*, I was especially struck by what Dr. Hayley Marama Cavino said: "One of our elders at home—Mereana Pitman—says that when you violate women and children you violate everyone, including yourself, because of the ways we are interconnected through genealogy. Sexual violence is never—for us—only about what happens to the individual, but rather is an assault against the blood—against our ancestors, our children to come, and all with whom we are connected in present time and place."

I believe that most people want justice, safety, and bodily autonomy—all of which include an end to intimate violence. But some hold on to the status quo. As I read article after article about intimate partner violence for this book, I thought, "We need a civil war—between feminists and patriarchs." Those on the side of the feminists are not only women, and those on the side of the patriarchs are not only men. I believe we are already in that war, which will lead to one of two possible outcomes: a world that is less safe for women or a world that is safer for women, especially women of color. I am fighting for the latter.

9

EXTRACTION

In September 2017, shortly before Eric and I broke up, a friend gifted me a visit to a medium, a person who communicates with the dead. She sent me because she wanted to do something nice for me and thought I would enjoy it. I had never been to a medium before. As a child in Sri Lanka, I had become accustomed to astrologers and psychics; that form of spirituality had been normal, but I had always taken it with a grain of salt. When I was young, my mother had had my horoscope read. I wish I still had that booklet with the predictions about my life. I remember it said I would become a doctor and have two children.

Going to the medium, as an adult, I was intrigued but skeptical. I had read Laura Lynne Jackson's *The Light Between Us: Stories from Heaven. Lessons for the Living*, about her experience as a medium. Jackson had worked with parents grieving the loss of a child and with law enforcement agents seeking clues to the location of the body of a murder victim. I kind of knew what to expect, but I wasn't prepared for the specificity of the reading.

Before I left to meet the medium, on a whim, I took three small photos I kept near my bed and put them into my backpack. They were of important people in my life who had died: my grandfather, my father, and a friend who had been killed by a hit-and-run driver when I was in high school. I believe that people who leave this earth still walk with us. I was curious how the presence of the three photos might impact what the medium saw.

Soon after she began, she asked, "Are you heartbroken?"

I responded, "I think so."

She talked about how she sensed that I had been knocked off my center. She felt a tensing in her chest. She told me to be really careful, to tiptoe through this time.

She said, "If it hasn't already, it's going to get a little messy." About the man in my life, she said, "I don't like him for you. There's a bigger situation here that's going to lead you out of this. I keep hearing the word *deafening*."

I had been experiencing a ringing in my ears. I didn't know where it had come from. I wondered if that was what she meant. "There's a very slight man who walks with you"—a man with the same physicality as me. She said that he was guiding me through this time. "It's your father."

Suddenly she said, "There's somebody showing me a necklace with a gold elephant on it. That's just a confirmation."

A few days before I had the reading, I had opened my jewelry drawer to find a gold chain to replace one that had broken. The necklace I had found was one I hadn't looked at in years, and it had a gold elephant on it. The drawer was just to the right of where the photos I put in my backpack had been.

After she mentioned the necklace, I settled in to receive everything she wanted to tell me.

"You're going to experience a detachment from things, to push them away, without the guilt, without the weight."

I told her, "I could potentially be in danger."

She said, "I don't like him. He's not well. He's not well, mentally." She talked about how he was a man of ego, charisma, and addiction. She said that any contact with him would rattle me right now and that I needed to be protected. She said to ghost him but to make it seem as though I was focusing on myself and my work.

I said, "As I piece together events in the last year, I see a lot of moments of abuse."

"This isn't going to get better. He does not have a turnaround in his future. You need to get help from people who know what you're going through." She said to make sure they were people who had no connection to him, that it couldn't get back to him what I was thinking.

I told the medium, "But I've also seen the softer side of him." I thought for a moment about the Eric I had met in Philadelphia who had seemed kind, sweet, and adoring.

"Fuck it. Don't worry about the soft side. You have the power; you have the information. The more people in your pod that know, the safer you are. When you tell someone about this sort of abuse, you make it less okay. You need to tell somebody what he did, and you need to see the reaction in their eyes. You need to let the air out of the balloon."

She talked about someone showing her a big bouquet of

bright flowers, a woman who left us earlier than she should have, a tall white woman with long white hair who bit her nails. That was my friend in the photo in my backpack.

"She's well. She's where she's supposed to be. She's also the one you can talk to during this time in particular. She's a totem for you. She wants you to plan a path to joy." She continued, "There's an honoring of the hurt that you're not very good at."

She told me to be careful about the stress of the road I was about to travel. Then she talked about a man surrounded by numbers who paid attention to the smallest details and used his hands a lot. That was my grandfather, a masterful accountant who folded his clothes meticulously. She said my grandfather wanted me to make the following lists:

People I would tell

People who would know what to do

Things that were better before my relationship

Things that I'd stopped myself from doing

Things I would tell the person I loved the
most if they were in my position

Things I wanted in a partner

She also told me to put on paper every remote trace of pain that I'd been through, even if I realized later on that I had seen it in the flash of an eye.

When I returned home, I sat at my desk and started the lists. For the things I would tell a person I loved the most who was in this position, I wrote:

Stay away.

There's nothing to be gained by confronting him.

Surround yourself with people who have your back.

Don't worry about those who don't have your back.

You are more important than him.

As I completed the lists, I sobbed.

Around that time, I got together with my longtime friend Danzy Senna, an author who was in town for the Brooklyn Book Festival. Over dinner, I told her about how things had been spiraling downward over the last many months with Eric. As I described the details of his abuse, she became disturbed. I told her that Eric was at a meditation retreat. She offered to go with me then and there to get all my belongings from his place. I had the keys; we could have done it. But I told her I wanted to wait. My things were not important.

The next day, I went to Los Angeles for a *Glamour* Women of the Year Awards shoot with Nicole Kidman, who in *Big Little Lies* plays a woman dealing with intimate violence in the sexual context. During the interview, as she said the words "domestic violence," my phone rang, displaying "No Caller ID." I knew it was Eric. It was a sign from the universe. I hadn't spoken with him since the week before, when I had stopped by his place to get my Massachusetts General Hospital ID card. I had already begun the process of drifting. What did he want? My body tensed up. My heart started palpitating.

He called twice more in the next twenty-four hours, increasingly agitated in his messages that he couldn't reach me.

He thought we were supposed to have dinner that week and wanted to confirm. By the third time he called, I thought it would make him crazy if I didn't respond, so I sent a short email to say that I was traveling and couldn't get together with him.

Meanwhile, I continued to speak with Jennifer Friedman. She kept reminding me that my safety, not his career, was paramount. She wasn't worried for my safety in public, but she recognized that I was on a slippery slope.

She said, "He's lived a double life for all these years. If you're alone with him, we don't know what he's capable of. I don't want you to be alone with him. Don't poke the bear."

Friedman and I talked about getting an order of protection, but Eric's prominent position made it impossible to do anything outside the public spotlight. She explained that as the attorney general of New York State, he would find out in three seconds if I filed a petition. She was really worried about my being alone with him because, she said, "that was always his MO." She cited the violence that happened during sex—always behind closed doors, only in very private spaces. Friedman and I both agreed that the purpose of an order of protection, to keep him away, would not necessarily solve the problems in my situation. She wanted me not to ruffle his feathers, to get out smoothly without alarming him. She encouraged me to slowly fade out of his life and treat it more like a normal breakup.

At the time, I had no desire to go public. I had my friends, my work, my family. Furthermore, I had my home, my own apartment. I had a place to escape to. I could focus on recovering and getting on with my life.

Eric really wanted to talk to me. Yom Kippur was about to

begin, and he wrote to me that he was going to use the period of atonement to reflect. After my conversations with Jennifer Friedman, I thought I could handle speaking with Eric and, moreover, use the opportunity to extricate myself. He and I set up a time for a call on October 1, after the end of Yom Kippur.

I consulted with Friedman about how to prepare. She told me not to say yes to anything that would involve seeing him, such as having dinner. She told me to say "I need to think about it." She warned me that he knew my strengths and weaknesses. Don't give away anything, she said. Don't be impulsive. Don't agree to go to his place by yourself. She wanted me to know that I was blameless, that his behavior was not my fault. He had made me feel responsible for his well-being. He might believe that I was responsible, but he had lived a long life before I had entered the picture. She said that I needed to be "unbrain-washed" of his psychological manipulation.

We came up with scripts for various scenarios. I'd been avoiding him for so many weeks that it would be odd if he hadn't picked up on where things were heading—that is, toward the end of our relationship. But she said he might initiate the breakup conversation, which would be ideal. That way, he would have agency over the situation. By giving him control, I could more easily extricate myself in such a way that he felt that he was his own boss and was still in charge of me. If that occurred, I could simply say "I think that's for the best."

If he didn't initiate the breakup, I could say "This just isn't working for me anymore" or "This isn't working for either one of us. It's not bringing out the best in either of us." If he tried to criticize me or the call took a negative turn, I should exit as quickly as possible.

"When people come at you, you get tongue-tied. It's a strategic way to manipulate and weaken you," she said.

She told me to be detached, be strong, and take control of the conversation. We decided that I could say "I recognize how hard this is for both of us, but I need to end the conversation" or "I'm sorry, I just can't have a conversation when you're criticizing me."

She wanted me to identify a friend I could see after I spoke with him, so that I wouldn't be alone.

When the time came for him to call, I calmed my nerves. I had a plan.

He started with "It seems like you've been avoiding me."

I responded, "I just need time."

He said that maybe we should go our separate ways.

I said the line I had practiced with Friedman: "I think that would be for the best."

He asked, surprised, "Really?"

I said, "Yes, I'll be fine."

Without drama, we agreed by phone to break up.

Four days later, the Harvey Weinstein story by Megan Twohey and Jodi Kantor broke in the *New York Times*. I felt a wave crash around me. The Me Too reckoning had begun. On October 10, when the *New Yorker* published its Weinstein story by Ronan Farrow, Eric emailed me, "When you can, I think we should talk. I want to continue to support your good work." I didn't think the timing was a coincidence.

That week, he wrote me twice more, first telling me that he would be away for the weekend if I wanted to come by and get my things and then asking if he should come with me to the *Glamour* Awards.

I responded, "Thank you for this offer. I am not going to get to that this weekend. I don't think it would be the best idea for you to come to the gala."

My situation was happening concurrently with developments in the national news cycle, and I felt overwhelmed by the convergence. I spoke with Jennifer Friedman, who said she had been thinking about me as the Weinstein news had erupted. She was still concerned about my safety. She asked about the security in my building. We talked again about an order of protection, but I felt that it would become public and there would be no way to protect my confidentiality. Also, I was not interested in ruining Eric's career. Friedman said that Eric's duplicity reminded her of that of Eliot Spitzer, the former governor of New York, who had resigned in disgrace over his solicitation of prostitutes.

We talked about how the next step would be to retrieve my belongings from Eric's apartment. Friedman had had twenty years of experience working with survivors; she understood the way an abuser's mind worked. I told her I still had the keys to Eric's apartment. Could I just go get everything when I knew he wouldn't be home? She wondered whether, if he came back to an empty apartment, he would fly off the handle. My stuff was not the most important thing; most important was being safe. She advised me against going over there anytime soon and said that when I did, I should make sure that a friend went with me.

I wrote in my journal:

If you want to kill me, go ahead. I've already faced death. You want to tap my phones? Fine. I already assumed all my communications are being tracked.

    You want to put me in jail? Go ahead.

Soon thereafter, Jennifer Gonnerman and I met for dinner on the Lower East Side. I hadn't seen her in a few months; she and her husband had had dinner with me and Eric early in our relationship. At that time, things had been good. Before Jennifer and I met up this time, I anticipated telling her what was going on. I wasn't sure how.

But she opened the door, asking "So is Eric going to send Harvey to jail?" She meant Weinstein.

I took a deep breath and said, "Jen, there's something I have to tell you that isn't easy." I knew what I had to do; I needed to tell her about Eric's abusive behavior. I was sorry I had not told her before. As an investigative reporter, she's heard many difficult stories. But I was her friend, not a subject. Toward the end, I mentioned that my next step would be to get my things at his place. She offered to come with me.

I wrote to Eric asking if I could come by that Friday. He said I could. I asked if I should leave the key with his doorman, but he said I didn't have to, that he would get it from me another time.

Jen and I worked quickly to round up my belongings. The book *On Tyranny: Twenty Lessons from the Twentieth Century*, by Timothy Snyder, was on the dining table. A framed tweet by Donald J. Trump attacking Eric, which Eric had received after he had appeared on *Late Night with Seth Meyers*, was nearby.

Jen told me to take photos of the different rooms in the apartment. She said that one day I might want to refer to them to spark details and memories of what had happened to me. As an investigative reporter, she knew the advice to give.

After we left the building and were waiting for a cab, with bags and bags of my things next to us on the sidewalk, she stopped and turned to me. We stared at each other for a moment. I felt a huge weight lifting off me. I had my things. I was closer to being free of him. Then she said, "You can't be the first person he has done this to. Someone doesn't just wake up in the morning and exhibit these behaviors."

THE PATTERN

11:11—that was the time on the clock as I walked through my front door after bringing my things back from his place. Whenever I see 11:11, I make a wish. That particular time, I wished to be safe.

The next morning, I received a text from Jennifer Gonnerman: "I have some info. Can you talk?" I called her right away. She was with a childhood friend of her husband. He just happened to be in town that day, and he was with her family in the park. Jennifer knew the friend had worked with an ex-girlfriend of Eric's. She didn't know if he and Eric's ex had been good friends or if they were still in touch, but she casually asked him if he had ever heard the ex say anything about Eric Schneiderman.

Without skipping a beat, the man talked about how while they had been dating, Eric had slapped her and spat at his friend in bed. He was still close with the woman, and he called her while Jennifer was on the phone with me. Jennifer conveyed the messages to me: Eric had told the woman to get Botox. He had insulted her ankles, saying they were thick. If they hadn't been, he said, she'd be really intimidating. It was a long time before me that she had been with him. She wanted me to know that I wasn't alone and I wasn't crazy. She also said to call her if I wanted to talk.

After I hung up with Jennifer, my heart dropped, and I felt panicked. He was going to do to someone else what he had done to that woman and to me. I felt a moral obligation to prevent that from happening. But how could I do so without putting myself into danger? Jennifer Friedman had made it clear that confronting him might set him off.

Another friend reached out to tell me that she had heard from a mutual friend about a woman who had used to work for Eric. The gist of it was that the woman had found him extremely creepy—always rescheduling an afternoon work meeting to an after-work drinks thing. He would be very suggestive in conversation, and she had been wary of him as a result.

I spent the next twenty-four hours intensely deliberating. I was part of a pattern: I was not the first, and I wouldn't be the last. It would be easier to drift away and not say anything. But that wouldn't be me. Discovering that others could be in danger marked a turning point. The silence of women before me meant that I had suffered, too, and silence didn't feel like an option I could live with. I felt that I was in a lose-lose situation.

Trauma can be so deafening at times that it becomes hard to think. In my case, the decision to fade away quietly and let Eric do his work conflicted with my desire to prevent him from harming another woman. I thought the world needed him to do a few more good things, such as stop Trump's travel bans and protect transgender people in the military. What made my situation complex and different was that my abuser was a liberal hero. I knew that people would doubt me and my motives. I knew that some would be angry with me for taking down one of their own progressive leaders. But Eric would not be the first hero to be a fraud, and I wanted to be the last woman he could harm.

After Eric and I broke up, a friend called to check on me.

"Why is it always these people who are so vocal that do these things?" he asked.

"It's like antigay people who turn out to be gay themselves," I answered. "Maybe it's because of self-loathing, because they need a mask over who they really are."

I appreciated the rage, sadness, and concern of my friends. I also appreciated the way they were able to see beyond my individual story to a larger societal problem. Over lunch with another friend, we talked about how Eric's whole platform was as a champion of women.

She said, "Isn't that always the case—those who are most staunch about an issue, whether it be women's rights or being antigay, turn out to be hiding something."

The disconnect between Eric's public persona and his private behavior resonated when I watched the documentary *Leaving Neverland*. It was triggering for me to hear Michael Jackson's victims talk about the ways in which they had been made to feel that his abuse was an expression of love, that they couldn't tell anyone or they'd be dead.

As my deliberation continued, I wrote a letter to Eric, knowing I would never send it:

I am recovering from a year+ of abuse by you. I don't expect you to acknowledge what you did. I don't even expect you to be aware of what you did. You were high on alcohol and Ambien much of the time. But a guy who hits me until I agree to do something I will never do, like find a young woman to have a three-way, or call him master or daddy, that's a sick guy. You are no better than Harvey Weinstein.

I'm not scared of you. Even though you said early on in our relationship that you would have to kill me if we broke up, that you could have my phone tapped and have me followed, I've already faced death, and it doesn't scare me. I can imagine that you would write me off as a crazy person. Well, I'm not. I have a lot of people who care about me privately and who knew about your controlling, demeaning treatment.

I had never been in an abusive relationship before, and I had never been with an alcoholic. Now I know. It's not okay how you treated me. You need help. I hope you get it.

The day after I found out about Eric's previous girlfriend, Jennifer Gonnerman and I spoke again. She wanted me to talk with a lawyer. She knew which one: Roberta "Robbie" Kaplan. She sent me a video of Kaplan speaking about marriage equality, which she had helped make a reality when she had represented the LGBTQIA+ activist Edith Windsor in the landmark 2013 Supreme Court case that had overturned the 1996 Defense of Marriage Act. Jennifer reached out to Kaplan on my behalf, and we arranged to speak by phone a few days later.

As I described my experiences with Eric to Kaplan, I could

hear her making noises as if she were disgusted. I thought her reactions were appropriate. She vocalized the disgust I was feeling. I told her that I didn't know what I was going to do but would keep her posted.

I called Jennifer Friedman to fill her in. I needed help figuring out the path forward. When I told her about the previous girlfriend, she said, "Now there's you and her. Others must be out there. He's been divorced for twenty years." We talked about the possibility of filing a police report, since over the course of a year this had been a pattern of behavior. She asked me to articulate one or two of the most memorable incidents. She said that criminal law gets into minutiae; the assertion had to be tight.

I said I wanted to keep a low profile. She talked about how coming forward and being safe were in conflict. If I chose to come forward, he would come after me publicly. If I didn't come forward, he would move on. But he would abuse his next girlfriend, too. Didn't I want to stop that?

I told her that I didn't see myself coming forward anytime soon. By laying out the abuse I dealt with, I would leave myself open to humiliation because of the publicity. However, I wouldn't feel good about myself if I didn't come forward. I knew what my goals would be: to warn other women, to get him to step down and get help, and to open up a conversation about intimate violence.

Friedman had a friend in a New York City district attorney's office. If I wanted an expert opinion, she said, she could speak to that person. If Eric's behavior became known, he would likely be investigated. Everyone would hold Eric's hand until they were told they couldn't. Certainly, some people had heard the rumors, but they had been just rumors. What was needed was for his victims to come out with facts.

I worried about widening the net of people who knew. I didn't want to risk the possibility of a journalist being tipped off. I imagined the media storm I would get caught up in. Considering my hesitation to come forward, Friedman and I decided that for the moment I would simply document everything. Unless I were willing to go to the police, she suggested, it would be unwise to do anything else. Her advice was to stay calm and be careful about whom I talked to.

Shortly thereafter, while in a cab, I saw an ad on the taxi's TV screen: "Reporting a sexual assault to the NYPD could lead to the perpetrator being brought to justice, future assaults being prevented, and connect you with important resources. The choice is yours."

Why didn't I go to the police? I didn't trust the process. I knew people who had had negative experiences with the police department when powerful men were involved. In my case, my abuser was the top law enforcement official in New York. If he had any inkling I was talking to the police, I was convinced he would come after me. Jennifer Friedman suggested that I meet with her and her mentor Dorchen Leidholdt, a survivors' rights advocate, to talk through everything. She felt that Leidholdt would provide solid, objective advice. I gave Friedman permission to speak with her about my situation. Friedman later told me that when she had explained to Leidholdt that there was a case involving a powerful New York State politician, Leidholdt had tried to guess who it was. She had named various men until she had gotten to Eric's name, and then it had clicked. She had thought it must be him. She had worked with Eric on strangulation legislation. She had felt that the pieces fit together; they made sense. He had put himself out there as such an ally of women.

We arranged to meet at Leidholdt's office, but then I received the address: 120 Broadway. That was the address of Eric's office. My heart dropped. I asked to change the location, and we met at a law firm elsewhere.

After hearing about my experience, Leidholdt said, "He's a sexual sadist." We talked about getting a restraining order. She looked at my correspondence with Eric and noted, in one exchange, that I had phrased carefully that I wanted him to respect my wishes not to communicate. She said that his continuing to reach out to me after such a request could be deemed stalking, which was illegal. But she made it clear to me that if I got a restraining order, the cat would be out of the bag before I had the chance to come forward, and he would try to silence me.

During a call with Robbie Kaplan, we spoke about filing a civil claim, in which case I would get a settlement. But I didn't want the money. I also looked into filing an ethics complaint. A friend knew someone who had worked on ethics issues in the attorney general's office. She trusted that person completely to keep it confidential and said she wouldn't disclose any identifying details. I told her to ask about the procedure. She reported back that she had gotten an answer she couldn't have anticipated: basically, the process of filing an ethics complaint was not guaranteed to be confidential, meaning that Eric might get wind of it before it was dealt with.

Another friend offered to connect me with a longtime friend who had been a top lawyer for New York State but was now in private practice. He could help me understand the kind of inquiry that might be initiated if there were stories about Eric being a perpetrator. But soon my friend called back to tell me that he was sorry, but the lawyer couldn't speak with me. He had worked with Eric before, so there was a conflict of interest. My heart dropped—another of the many times it had been dropping as revelations and coincidences piled up. I became deeply scared. I felt for the first time that it might get back to Eric what I was contemplating doing. I started shaking as I hung up the phone. A few minutes later, I called my friend. I wanted reassurance that my story would be safe. My friend said he hadn't given my name.

I threw myself into my work and spent time with a close circle of friends. In those days, after I found out about Eric's previous girlfriend, I was knee-deep in producing content for the *Glamour* Women of the Year Awards. One day, I got together with a designer friend who was loaning me a dress for the ceremony. The first thing he said was, "I'm so sorry about you and Eric."

I asked, "How do you know?" I had told only a handful of people about the breakup.

He said that Eric had reached out to him about having dinner. My friend had thought he was going to see both of us, as he usually did, and had been surprised when I wasn't there. When he had asked Eric how I was doing, Eric had told him we had split. Later in the dinner, Eric had asked our friend to introduce him to women. He'd said it was hard for him to meet people in the type of work that he did.

I gasped. Eric was going to do to another woman what he had done to me, and I wanted to stop that from happening. But I still didn't know how.

At the *Glamour* Women of the Year Summit (a day of panels and performances that preceded the awards ceremony), I heard woman after woman on the stage talk about the Me Too movement and the importance of speaking up. Sheila Nevins, then the president of HBO Documentary Films, talked about how the traditional rules of the game had been that women slept with their bosses. Cameron Russell, the model, talked about how the highest compliment given to a model was "She'll do anything." When Russell had been starting out, she had been told that she would have trouble getting booked because she was a virgin.

On the way to the awards ceremony that night, I saw a sign on a bus stop for a show on Comedy Central. The tagline was "Trust no one." At the event, the journalists Megan Twohey and Jodi Kantor of the *New York Times* spoke from the podium about their uncovering of the Weinstein story. A group of survivors including Aly Raisman, the Olympic gymnast who was part of the Sister Army that had taken down sports doctor Larry Nassar, and Anita Hill took the stage. We all stood and clapped and cried. As the applause continued, Anita Hill looked up and around at the crowd. She lifted her arms slightly, as if she were finally receiving the support that she had deserved for decades.

By coincidence, during the dinner afterward I was seated next to Megan Twohey. I expressed my admiration for her. I held on to my big secret, but I did say to her that there were many powerful perpetrators who needed to be exposed.

She said, "It seems like you have something to get off your chest."

A few weeks after the *Glamour* Awards, I told Cindi Leive,

then the editor in chief of *Glamour*, in whom I had already confided, that I felt I was getting closer to knowing what I wanted to do. I had explored so many legal pathways for stopping Eric's cycle of abuse, but they had all seemed connected to him in some way. It was really the court of public opinion that might be my best shot. I told her that I was going to Portland for a few weeks; there I would reflect on my decision, and I would reconnect with her after I returned.

The day I left for Portland, December 26, there was a feature about Eric in the *New York Times*: "New York's Attorney General in Battle with Trump." My eyes opened wide when I got to this part: "Certainly, Mr. Schneiderman and Mr. Trump have little in common. Mr. Trump watches a lot of TV and craves his McDonald's. Mr. Schneiderman does yoga. 'Other than sports, I really don't watch TV much anymore,' Mr. Schneiderman said." But he had watched TV every night while I was trying to fall asleep.

The month before, Samantha Bee had done a special segment with Eric on her show, *Full Frontal with Samantha Bee*, that included a cartoon of him as Spiderman, except he was "Schneider-Man." A friend emailed me, "Hi Tanya. Hope all is well! Was watching Samantha Bee last night, and lo and behold there is Schneider-Man. Hilarious, and, as far as politicians go, he is definitely a superhero."

GQ ran a profile about Eric: "New York Attorney General Eric Schneiderman on What It Takes to Keep Trump in Check." The subhead was "A conversation with the man who has been a thorn in the president's side for years." Eric was quoted as saying "There are always those who will seek to undermine and discredit our work, but as the people's lawyer, you get used to that."

As I made my way to Portland, I thought, "This is what I'm up against."

A few months before I had met Eric, in the summer of 2016, an enormous tree had fallen on my house in Portland. I spend time there in large part because of the trees. They calm me. I can stare at them for hours. They are majestic, prehistoric, and inspiring. I think the trees and nature of Portland contribute to its reputation as a great city for writers. Luckily, the tree had damaged only an exterior part of the house. Skilled arborists and contractors had put everything back together.

After Eric and I broke up, I was telling a friend about the falling of the tree. She lived in northern California, and her husband was a firefighter who had dealt with some of the biggest wildfires in US history. She believed in the symbolism of trees. She asked me what kind of tree it was. When I said it was a big-leaf maple, she told me that it's a tree much revered for its canopy, protection, and sweetness, that its wood is used in wands and charms of protection. She said the tree might have been (a) trying to get my attention and (b) offering medicine. She felt my relationship with Eric was like the falling of the tree: a shaking of my foundation, but the house was okay. The damage could be fixed.

Like trees, books often intersect with my life. When I was writing my first book, Sonali Deraniyagala's memoir, *Wave*, appeared. She wrote about losing generations of her family—her parents, her children, and her husband—in the December 2004 tsunami in Sri Lanka, yet she ended the book, stunningly, on a note of hope. On keeping her family alive and close around her even after they were gone, she said, "More and more now I keep my balance while staring into us. And I welcome this, a small triumph, it lights me up." I thought that if she could go on, then I must, too.

As I was deciding whether to come forward, I read *When Women Were Birds* by Terry Tempest Williams, who wrote, "To withhold words is power. But to share our words with others, openly and honestly, is also power."

When I was in Portland, I treated those weeks as though they might be my last on Earth. I spent New Year's Eve watching my friends' band Pink Martini play at Schnitzer Hall. I felt huge gratitude for my friends there and everywhere, for my home, for my career. In addition to *Glamour*, I had started collaborating with Planned Parenthood and was in the beginning stages of developing a new campaign that would ultimately be titled "Unstoppable." The title was inspired by a speech that Cecile Richards, then the president of Planned Parenthood, had given at the first Women's March, in January 2017. She had said, "One of us can be dismissed, two of us can be ignored, but together, we are a movement, and we are unstoppable."

After I returned to New York, I met with Cindi Leive and told her I had made my decision. I was scared, but I was ready to have a conversation with David Remnick. Because of the respect I had for the *New Yorker* and because of its courageous Me Too reporting, I felt that my story would be safe with him. That weekend he and I emailed each other, and we set up a time to speak.

COMING FORWARD

Before I met with David Remnick, I let him read my first-person anonymous narrative about my experience. It was about fifteen pages long. I also sent it to a trusted friend who knew I was exploring coming forward. She sent me an email:

> His behavior is even worse and more repulsive than I imagined. I am so enraged that he inflicted this on you. I'm enraged that he acted like a righteous women's advocate when he's so clearly filled with anger toward them. The slave talk is shockingly racist. I remember early on, when you first told me that he criticized your hair and clothes and didn't like you talking on the phone—it felt ominous and reminded me of the way my stepfather acted toward my mother. I remember those times you told me how severe his drinking is, and I told you that you seemed subdued in the relationship. I wish I would have read between the lines earlier. I looked up the signs of a domestic abuser after I read this, and so much of it is embodied here.

I'm so, so sorry that you endured this for a year and so proud
that you want to protect other women.

I was moved by how fully she grasped my experience. I especially appreciated that she picked up on the racism inherent
in Eric's treatment of me. I was sorry that she was sorry. But
really, how could she or any of my friends have been able to
read between the lines as long as I wasn't telling them what
was happening?

Remnick spoke with a few friends of mine at the *New Yorker*
to get their opinion of me. One of them was Jennifer Gonnerman. She told him that she'd known me for more than twenty
years, that she had gone with me to get my things from Eric's
place, and that within twenty-four hours she had found a previous girlfriend who had recounted a similar experience with him.

When Remnick and I got together at a café, he made it clear
that our conversation would be confidential and off the record,
that it was preliminary and between us alone. He said that he
had read my first-person account and asked me what I wanted
to do. I said that if the *New Yorker* was interested in pursuing
the story, I would participate. He admitted that a first-person
story would be tough, because it was a "he said, she said" situation and hard to fact-check unless there were photos or a police
report. I told him I didn't have that kind of evidence. Also,
although Eric had slapped me hard, he had never given me a
black eye, and on my dark skin, slap marks were less likely to
be visible.

I wondered, "Do I need to have gotten a black eye to be
believed?"

We agreed that I would be even more careful about telling anyone and that I would give him time to think about what to do.

That was mid-January. I was still working in the Condé Nast building, One World Trade Center. Soon after I met with Remnick, I saw him in the Condé Nast cafeteria while I was with a friend who worked at the *New Yorker*. Remnick waved, and I waved back, but my friend didn't notice. I didn't know if I was supposed to acknowledge him or not. I saw him again that same week. Synchronicity is a curious thing. I'd been going to that dining room for about seven months, but only after I got together with Remnick did I see him there twice in one week.

Soon thereafter, I received an email from Eric: "T, I am trying to get backstage passes to the Grammys on Sunday night, feb 28. Would you like to come as my plus 1? Of all the people I know, it seems right to take you."

When he reached out to me, aside from feeling sick, I had two thoughts: (1) He wasn't seeing anyone, so he wasn't abusing someone else, which I found reassuring. (2) He didn't know what I was thinking.

I hadn't heard from him in a few months, and to hear from him then dragged me back into fear. I felt my insides shake. I responded, "I don't think that would be a good idea."

I was about to go to Los Angeles to attend the Makers Conference, which celebrates women's stories and achievements. Before I went, I thought about the previous girlfriend. I knew she lived in LA. I looked her up online and went to her Twitter page. To my surprise, she was following me. I decided to send her a direct message, simply saying that I was going to be in

LA if she had any time. She wrote back right away with her number. I planned to text her after I arrived.

In LA, I visited Danzy Senna. We hadn't seen each other since she had been in New York to speak at the Brooklyn Book Festival many months before. This time, she told me that she had been so freaked out by what I had described to her about Eric that she had written a record of our conversation and emailed it to herself and her husband. She remembered asking me if I knew of other women he had done this to. Back then, I hadn't. She remembered that I had told her Eric was at some New Age retreat and that she had wanted to go with me right then and there to get my things from his place. She said that I was one of her oldest friends, and she was worried that something bad would happen to me. She said she kept thinking about Nicole Brown Simpson, O.J.'s murdered wife.

I paused to take that in. Then I told her that I was thinking about coming forward.

She said, "The most important thing is you're out. You're safe and seem better than ever."

A day later, I texted Eric's previous girlfriend, and we arranged to meet at a café. I arrived first and sat at a table in the back.

When she got there, she asked, "Is this okay for you?"

I responded, "Is it for you?"

She said it felt as though we were on display, so we walked outside through a parking lot to a bench that overlooked a lower parking lot. After we sat down, the stories poured out of her. She shared my sense that when he had first slapped her during sex, it was as if he were testing her. From there, the abuse had escalated. He would hold up her leg admiringly and then say she had thick ankles. He would touch her eyes, stretch out the skin around them, and say she needed Botox. He had asked her to find women for three-ways. When she had confronted him about his treatment of her, he had said that she wasn't sexually liberated and that she was depriving him of his needs. She described him as a master of psychological manipulation. She talked about the meditators he surrounded himself with. She had wanted him to see a therapist with her. He had found one, whom he had paid under the table, and the therapist had told her that she was overreacting.

At one point I looked for my phone to check the time. She looked worried and asked if I was recording our conversation. I said no. She wondered if anyone was surveilling us. I found it striking that she felt that level of fear so long after her involvement with Eric had ended. I reassured her that we were alone. She began again: "He toyed with my heart."

She said he had tried to position himself as a good guy and someone who cared. He was politically liberal and attractive. "The optics of it looked so good." She had thought she might become Mrs. Schneiderman.

She said she had lost a lot of weight. She had known that if she stayed, she would become a skeleton of herself. Of the end, she said, "I'd had enough."

I felt as if I were hearing her tell me my own story, except it was hers.

After they had broken up, she had told a few people about her experience with him. She had told people in political circles. She said there were definitely rumors going around about Eric's behavior. She had been approached a few times by reporters, and she had considered exposing him but was scared. Some people had told her to keep quiet. Instead, she had written out her account and put it into a safe-deposit box in case anything happened to her. She had given the key to two friends. She felt alone and silenced by fear. At the time, she had trodden softly. She said that to this day she hadn't been able to open her heart to anyone. She said she wanted her true self back. She said times had changed—referring to the Me Too movement.

A few years before, she had heard through a friend about a woman who had dated Eric and talked about him slapping her around. The woman had abruptly ended the relationship. I told her that in abusing me, Eric had messed with the wrong woman. I told her I was thinking about coming forward. She didn't know if she would be able to join me, but she told me she would say, "I believe Tanya one hundred percent."

The time had come for me to go to the Makers Conference. We hugged and parted ways. Later, when we spoke on the phone, she said that normally after talking about him, she felt fear, but not after talking to me. She also said, "I feel protective of you."

I began to feel that I had to come forward, not only for the women who might date him after me but for that woman, too.

She told me, "In you is a bit of a savior. You are the answer to a question."

I wasn't sure how to respond. I didn't want to make too much of the part I was about to play.

The theme of the Makers Conference was "Raise Your Voice." I heard woman after woman talk about the changing times. As I listened to Marcia Clark, the prosecutor in the O. J. Simpson trial, I thought about Danzy referencing Nicole Brown Simpson. I went to a talk by Gloria Steinem and Amy Richards at which Amy, a longtime friend, said that the Simpson trial had been the moment when people had first heard about domestic violence in a very public way.

Everywhere I turned at the conference, there was a story of abuse. One speaker said that victims needed to know that if they spoke out, there would be no retaliation against them. But I thought to myself, as I often did, "What do you do if your abuser is the top law enforcement official in your state?"

Time's Up had recently begun, and many of the women involved in it participated in the conference. In the audience was Robbie Kaplan, the lawyer with whom I had spoken on the phone a few months before. She had become the cofounder of the TIME'S UP Legal Defense Fund. Amy Richards introduced us. Kaplan and I simply said hi and made no allusions to our previous conversation.

Around that time, I had a dream about trying to hide my first-person narrative from Eric. I was still with him, but I had hidden the hard copy in a backpack in a closet. He returned home. He was like a child. He wanted me to take care of him. He wanted me to have sex with him. I didn't want to, but I also felt as though doing it would make him less likely to find my essay. While he went to the bathroom, I worried that he might open the closet. I rushed to take the piece out of the backpack and tried to figure out where to put it. Then, suddenly, I was not in his apartment but in a house with many levels. It was a very narrow building. I opened an exit door, and there were no stairs, just a slope. I slid all the way from the top of the house to the ground floor.

When I woke, I opened a news app on my phone and saw Eric's face. His photo was the thumbnail for an article on Politico about Democratic attorneys general. It cited him as aspiring to be governor of New York.

I was preparing to leave for Sri Lanka that day when the Rob Porter story broke about how he, the White House staff secretary, had a pattern of abusing his intimate partners. Jennifer Willoughby, his second wife, described him as "a man who could be both charming and romantic and fun—and even thoughtful and kind; and horribly angry and manipulative." The White House had known about the allegations as early as January 2017 but had allowed Porter to keep his job. Dahlia Lithwick wrote a piece for *Slate* titled "Rob Porter's History of Domestic Abuse Wasn't a Secret. It's Just That No One Cared."

I received a few texts, including from Jennifer Friedman, wanting to know how I was doing. My friends were worried about how the news would affect me, but I felt a strengthening. I felt a door opening. Against the backdrop of Me Too, the press was finally talking about domestic violence. Lithwick cited Catharine MacKinnon's op-ed about Me Too for the *New York Times*:

It typically took three to four women testifying that they had been violated by the same man in the same way to even begin to make a dent in his denial. That made a woman, for credibility purposes, one-fourth of a person.

Even when she was believed, nothing he did to her mattered as much as what would be done to him if his actions against her were taken seriously. His value outweighed her sexualized worthlessness.

I knew that coming forward publicly would be my best chance at effecting change. I also recognized the possibility in my story for increased public awareness and education around intimate violence. If Eric hadn't been an important, powerful man, no one would care.

Soon after I arrived in Sri Lanka, my grandmother—my mother's mother—asked a lot of questions about Eric, whom she mistakenly called "Ned."

"What happened?"

I responded, "He was controlling."

"You used to like him."

"But then he started to be more controlling. He wanted me to dress a certain way, do my hair a certain way. I couldn't be free."

Suddenly she asked, about my father, "Did he hit Mummy?"

"Yes."

"Often?"

"Yes."

"Did you see it?"

"Yes. He was Jekyll and Hyde."

"And Ned, was he also Jekyll and Hyde?"

"Yes."

She asked if he had hit me. We just stared at each other.

My grandmother had always impressed me with her strength and forcefulness. She didn't suffer fools; she stood up for herself. My grandfather was the quiet, mild one. My grandmother was sometimes referred to as a "hurricane." There wasn't a long-standing generational cycle of violence in my family. That cycle began with my mother, and I was determined for it to end with me.

After a pause, my grandmother said, "At that time, I was happy for you. But then you found you had a big frog."

She told me she was tired and wanted to sleep. I went downstairs to my bedroom and opened my computer to find an email from Eric: "Sorry to bother you. But I need to speak with you about a sensitive matter. When is a good time to speak?"

I wrote simply that I was traveling and with my family.

He wrote again: "This will be brief, but is time sensitive if you have 3 minutes for a telephone call. I would not bother you if it was not important."

I started shaking, feeling the rapid palpitations of my heart that I had come to recognize so well. Context is as important as or more important than content. The timing of when Eric reached out to me spoke volumes. He had been keeping up appearances, but the seams were beginning to rip.

Aside from the Rob Porter story, it was all over the news about Eric filing a lawsuit against the Weinstein Company and blocking its sale. Many leading figures in the Me Too and Time's Up movements thanked him publicly. Eric was once again positioning himself as their hero. Andrew Ross Sorkin wrote in the *New York Times* that when Eric held a news conference about the case, "he spoke at a lectern with the words 'Justice for Victims' written across it."

Eric appeared on PBS's *Frontline* to talk about how he was holding Weinstein accountable. To me, he seemed to have a Weinstein-level pathology, as if he were purposely provoking a media person to dig. Around that time, he spoke at an event called "Fight Back like a Girl," hosted by the women's health nonprofit Lady Parts Justice League and the political organizing platform #VOTEPROCHOICE. When the *New Yorker* and the *New York Times* shared the 2018 Pulitzer Prize for Public Service for their Me Too coverage, Eric tweeted, "Without the reporting of the @nytimes and the @newyorker—and the brave women and men who spoke up about the sexual harassment they endured at the hands of powerful men—there would not be the critical national reckoning underway. A well-deserved honor."

I thought, "He's writing the story for me."

While I was in Sri Lanka, I didn't tell anyone in my family what was happening, that I had been in an abusive relationship and was thinking of coming forward. I felt that if I told one person, the whole family would find out. And if that happened, then all of Sri Lanka would know.

I thought about a friend who had recalled, after Eric and I broke up, my telling her about how he wouldn't let me eat meat in front of him and how he wanted me in his apartment but wouldn't come to mine. She had said that that type of controlling behavior of a woman in her forties was not normal. Before I left Sri Lanka, my aunt, who had cooked a lavish spread to welcome Eric when he had been there with me the year before, pulled me aside. She put her arm around me and whispered, "Now you can eat chicken."

On the plane back from Sri Lanka, it hit me how far away I had gotten from everything in the United States and how close I could be to having my privacy and life disrupted for some time. After I returned to New York, David Remnick and I spoke, and he told me that he had decided to assign a reporter to the story. At the moment, she was working on a big piece, so he would speak with her after she had turned it in.

He said, "You know a lot of people. Don't tell anyone about this."

It was going to be the scariest thing I had ever done. I had been in Sri Lanka during curfews and bomb threats. I had gotten onto a plane a few days after 9/11. The bones in my chest had been sawed through to remove a tumor. But this was different. This involved putting out intimate details about myself. I felt embarrassed and ashamed that my sex life would be exposed and that people might see that before they saw me. I valued my freedom, my ability to escape and be unbothered. I wished that I could come forward without my name being disclosed. I vacillated between wanting to hide and go underground and wanting to go public and make sure this never happened to anyone else.

I considered moving and went and looked at a few apartments. I loved my building, but it was hard to hide there. With a central courtyard flanked by entryways, it was a fishbowl where everyone could see my comings and goings. I tried to go about my business as usual. I participated in a panel at the Athena Film Festival at Barnard College. I decided to walk home as much of the way as possible. For the first time since I had gotten my things from Eric's place, I was on the Upper West Side. I considered walking toward the area near his building, to conquer my fear. But I felt sick. I wondered if I should get out of town and stay out.

In early March, Remnick and I spoke again, and he told me the reporter would be Jane Mayer. Her other story would be running soon. The second week of March, her explosive piece about the Steele dossier (which contained allegations of misconduct and conspiracy between Trump and Russia) came out. On March 19, she sent me an email to set up a time to talk. We arranged to speak the next day.

That night, I went to a small birthday dinner that Amy Richards was hosting for me. The guests all knew what I was dealing with. I felt as though it was my last supper. I gave a toast and said that birthdays were not simply markers of being a year older but markers of knowing people longer and that friends made my world go 'round.

On March 20, my actual birthday, I spoke with Mayer, and Robbie Kaplan (who was now officially my lawyer) was on the call, too. I told Mayer, "I am honored, grateful, and nervous to be talking to you." Mayer had cowritten the book *Strange Justice: The Selling of Clarence Thomas*, about Anita Hill and Clarence Thomas. She had also written *Dark Money*, the book about the Koch brothers that was prominently displayed in Eric's apartment.

I described my experience to her as I had done with Robbie and with Remnick. As I got to the end, I told her, "He's going to try to kill me or have someone try to kill me."

She said, "He won't kill you. Well, I think if we get three women to talk on the record, he's over. Robbie, don't you think so?"

Robbie responded, "I think you're right."

Later that day, I left for Portland. After I settled into my house, I tried to open a box that had been delivered. The knife I was using slipped and pierced the skin between my thumb and index finger. I started bleeding profusely. I rinsed the wound and applied multiple bandages. When I woke up the next morning, it was still bleeding. I went to the emergency room. The doctor told me I was lucky I hadn't hit a nerve or tendon. As my hand healed, I reminded myself to stay grounded in my actions and aware of my surroundings.

Over the next few days, I continued to speak with Mayer. During one conversation, she asked, "Why does the public need to know this?"

I answered, "He holds himself out as a feminist and the highest legal authority on equality in the state."

She said, "Yes, it's relevant to voters to know if he really is. But JFK turned out not to be a great guy."

While running errands, I noticed an AT&T store and spontaneously stopped in. I asked the salesperson about a nontraceable phone. I told her I was producing a project that contained sensitive information.

She said, "Like a throwaway phone?"

"Yes."

"We have a lot of women who come in and need phones that aren't attached to their name and number."

I wondered what kind of work the women did. Were they drug dealers or spies?

While she was setting up the phone for me, another salesperson, who had heard me reference my work making movies, talked about how he wanted to be an actor but didn't want to risk moving to Hollywood. He liked having a roof over his head. He liked the outdoors.

It was a perfect sunny day.

After an hour and a half, I was still there. They were having technical difficulties creating my account. We joked about making a documentary called *System Failure*.

When the process was finally complete, the supervisor apologized and said to me, "Happy Easter."

I asked if she needed anything else.

She said, "I just need you to be happy for me the rest of the night. You take care always."

The unsolicited kindness of a stranger in that moment moved me.

I began to feel as though the time had come to prepare important people in my life for the story to come out. I had lunch with a friend and asked, "Am I doing the right thing?"

She said, "You know in your heart of hearts you are. You don't have a choice."

I called Carrie Mae Weems to let her know. Carrie had witnessed the beginning of the relationship.

She said, "I'm scared for you. You have a home at my place."

She asked, "Have you heard from Knucklehead?"

I said I had received a few emails from him insisting that we talk.

She said, "I don't know whom to trust." Knowing what Eric had done to me and other women, she was horrified by his speaking out against Weinstein.

I called another friend. She was concerned that if my story became public, I wouldn't be able to control the narrative. She wondered if it would be better to take the mic myself and say, "This is what happened to me." She said that it was an incredibly important and powerful story but I should be prepared for a libel suit, that I should marshal a support group of her and other friends.

I called my brother and sister-in-law. My brother warned me about being named. He said, "You might not be happy with having been on the record after it comes out. So many women's lives are ruined after they out an abuser." But they both said that they supported me and offered me a hiding place in their house.

I spoke with my mother. "I want to talk to you about something. It's not an easy conversation to have."

I took deep, quiet breaths. I felt that if I could model clarity and calm for my mother, I would be more likely to receive the same from her. I was seated at my desk, the same desk where I do most of my writing. It was daytime and gray, which was not unusual around that time of year, early spring. I prepared myself to speak directly and hoped that my mother would listen.

I described how Eric had slapped me, belittled me, and tried to control me. I told her that I was not the only one he had done that to, and it seemed likely to become public. After I finished, she sounded weirdly relieved. "I thought you were going to tell me the cancer had come back, and *that* I wouldn't have been able to take."

She started talking about my father. She said that when he had been dying from lung cancer, "Daddy told your uncle he was suffering because of what he did to me." She went on about my father, "I hate him. I hate him." A few seconds later: "I don't hate him. I sometimes feel . . . I'm glad he's dead and gone. I had twenty-four years of suffering. Now twenty-four years since he died. After seeing what happened to me, you should have left after the first time."

I said, "I know, and now I know forever." After a pause, I said, "When it started happening, it was jarring and scary. I thought it was specific to me. I thought he was having a breakdown."

"He will get what's coming to him. You don't have to do it."

I said, "He's been getting away with it for a long time. And he will continue to unless I do something."

She said she didn't want me to come forward. "I don't want publicity."

I said, "I need support."

I was glad she hadn't freaked out. I said I was sorry for what I had had to tell her but thanked her for listening. That conversation was one of the most candid my mother and I had ever had with each other. I felt a huge sense of relief that I wasn't keeping the secret from her anymore. I felt that she had heard me about needing support.

But a few hours later, she called again. "You should never have stayed with him after the first time. He thought he was a big shot. It's your mistake for not walking. When I see him, I will spit on his face. Because he's the attorney general, people kowtow to him. He thought he's a big deal. We're a bigger deal."

I recognized that my experience was triggering for her, with regard to her abuse by my father and the inability of many in her family to accept her truth. From time to time, I go back in my mind to that moment of telling my mother, especially when I'm sitting at the desk where I write. The memory makes me sad. But I did what I had to do. I had no choice. I was left with no alternative that made sense or felt true to who I am.

12

THE ROLLER COASTER

In less than two weeks after I first spoke with Jane Mayer, she connected with several other ex-girlfriends of Eric and listened to their stories, which were strikingly similar to mine. She had the material she needed to build a piece, and she wanted to publish it as soon as possible. I told her I needed time to get my life together. I needed to get back to New York and make plans for my security and escape. I knew that without my participation, there would be no story. But I felt terrible telling her that I wasn't ready for the story to be public yet. I emailed her that I needed a week.

She tried to reach me by phone many times, and when she eventually did, she said, "Are you sure you need to worry this much? It's not that difficult to stay safe. I've covered two wars—you can do this." But I told her I couldn't return to New York into a maelstrom. I asked her to give me time.

Although I had no children, I worried about the impact that coming forward would have on my extended family and on my career and reputation. Once I put my story out there, I wouldn't be able to take it back, and I couldn't anticipate how my life would change. I kept reminding myself that my friends and my work were solid and would still be there for me. A few people might drift away, and that would be okay. I had a handful of friends who had told me not to do anything, but they were outnumbered by those who had told me that I knew what I had to do. When the history of Me Too would be written, I wouldn't be able to live with being the one who had been too scared to protect other women.

The news cycle would pass, and then no one would care anymore. In a few years, no one might remember Eric's name. I didn't expect him ever to acknowledge the harm he had done to me, the ways in which he had eroded my self-esteem. I had to fight against my own disappointment that the women before me could have prevented him from doing that to me. It became clear during the reporting of the story that previous girlfriends had told themselves to stay silent or had people telling them not to do anything.

I spoke with a friend who taught at a university that was dealing with its own reckoning over a professor who had harassed colleagues and students. She talked about how Eric was a high-profile guy with many opportunities to meet women. She encouraged me to go on the record in order to minimize the access he had to women he could abuse. She said the story was becoming a many-headed monster, and not every part would turn out the way I wanted it to, but she agreed that I would be doing the right thing.

When *Time* magazine named "The Silence Breakers" its 2017 Person of the Year, it conducted an online poll showing that "82% of respondents said women are more likely to speak out about harassment since the Weinstein allegations." Eighty-five percent said that they "believe the women making allegations of sexual harassment."

In early April, a woman testified under oath that Eric Greitens, then the governor of Missouri, had sexually coerced and abused her. Pressure mounted for him to resign. Around that time, I received an email from Eric. Because I wasn't responding to him, he replied twice to his own email, increasing the urgency. The tone felt similar to that of the emails he had sent while I was in Sri Lanka, insisting we had to talk, then becoming angry that I wouldn't.

He wrote, "I thought we parted with a high degree of mutual respect, but I guess I was wrong." In his next email, he claimed he had to talk to me about Weinstein. He wanted to know if Weinstein had donated money to the films I had been producing around the election. In 2016, Eric had in fact mentioned to Weinstein the work I was producing, and Weinstein had said he wanted to support it. But he had never donated to it. To stop the email train, I responded with a simple "No."

I showed the emails to Jennifer Friedman. She said that Eric kept showing his true colors, which she found weirdly reassuring. "You don't even have to push him that hard. He's totally clueless and lacks self-awareness. A normal person would say, 'Hey, is something wrong?' They wouldn't lash out. They would be concerned."

When I was back in New York, I was able to focus on preparing for the day the story would come out. Amy Richards urged me to get security training, and she connected me with security expert Gavin de Becker's team. They counseled me on my safety and provided me with recommendations.

At some point before the story came out, Eric would hear about it. I felt the gravity of the risk I would be taking. I thought about the many women who had been sharing their Me Too stories and wondered what precautions they had taken to safeguard their security.

Among the first precautions I took was to remove my name from the buzzer list and my mailbox at my building. I also deleted my social media accounts. The social media life was never for me anyway. Shortly before my first book had come out, my publicist had encouraged me to join all platforms, but it had never felt quite right. It had been wonderful reconnecting with friends from college, high school, and even elementary school. Other than that, I didn't need social media. After I deleted my accounts, I was more curious about people because I didn't already know what they were up to. I liked them more because I wasn't being constantly updated about the mundane details of their lives.

On April 25, I met Jane Mayer for dinner in my neighborhood on the Lower East Side. We spent about three hours together. I found her easy to talk to, but I kept reminding myself that she wasn't my friend. It's the skill of the best reporters to be likable and make the subject feel liked. At one point, I told her, "I wish my name didn't have to be mentioned." But I submitted myself to the process of journalism.

She asked if I would be amenable to allowing the article to include the photo of a bruised Eric in the hospital the day before the president's inauguration. I said I needed to think about it. I knew that I was fine with the photo being described, but

I wasn't comfortable with it being shown. I felt it would be all over the tabloids in a second. I had straightforward objectives that didn't require extreme measures to be achieved. But I had the image on my phone, so I decided to let her see it.

The next day, Mayer and I met at Robbie Kaplan's office, where we were joined by Ronan Farrow, who had recently been added as a reporter on the investigation. He and Mayer had not collaborated before, and he was helping with the correspondence with the women who would potentially participate. He also had leads on other women with similar stories.

Mayer and Farrow had me tell my story from beginning to end, and they occasionally asked questions. I was getting used to the telling and retelling. I recognized it as an important part of the process, which I was focused on supporting.

I remember being struck by both Mayer's and Farrow's calm composure, gentle listening, and clear reasoning. I felt that I was in the best possible hands and that the outcome was now out of my hands. It had taken Farrow a year to get women on the record about Weinstein. With this case, it had taken a matter of weeks.

As we walked out of the office, Farrow thanked me. He also said, "You might want to turn off your phone for a while when this comes out."

Afterward, at a work meeting, four breaking news alerts popped up on my phone: Bill Cosby had been convicted.

I said to those in the meeting, "That would not have happened a year ago."

My story, I knew, could drop any day. The question was: With which women participating? First there was me, then there were three, then there were two, now there might be four.

Would Mayer and Farrow hear back from a fifth? In those final days, the number was going up and down and all around.

And then there was a leak. To the *New York Times*. A reporter there was trying to reach other previous girlfriends of Eric's. About a week later, the reporter emailed Robbie Kaplan and then called her with a tactless message that she'd heard that Robbie had a client with a Me Too story about Eric Schneiderman.

I wrote to Robbie, "She's got no story if no one talks to her."

I decided I didn't need to hide yet, but I wanted to escape my thoughts, so I went gallery hopping. I visited Hank Willis Thomas's exhibition *What We Ask Is Simple*, in which he depicted historical images of protests and the civil rights movement. In one piece, a sign read, "Men of quality are not threatened by women for equality."

The Tribeca Film Festival was on, and I went to a screening of *RX: Early Detection—A Cancer Journey with Sandra Lee* and the reception afterward. Governor Andrew Cuomo was there to support his then partner Sandra Lee's premiere. I was overwhelmed by the secret I was keeping inside. I couldn't help but think that Cuomo knew what was brewing with regard to Eric.

I hadn't eaten. I had a bourbon. It went to my head. I went home. As I walked toward the entryway of my building, I lost my footing and fell. It's embarrassing to lose one's step in public.

I started to anticipate the fallout after Mayer and Farrow's story came out. The race the *New York Times* was now imposing would accelerate the story's release. I thought it would be Eric's word against mine.

He would say that he remembered things differently. Mem-

ory and experience can be subjective. There are often two real-
ities, the victim's and the abuser's, but one is telling the truth
and one is trying to squash it. In this case, several women very
different from one another and interviewed independently were
telling similar stories. I felt that objectivity would emerge.

It wasn't just the exposing of the story that frightened me
but also the scrutiny of my personal life. When people met
me, that story might be the first thing they associated with
me. When they googled me, it might be the result they noticed
most. I expected these reactions: "She's being an opportunist."
"She stayed with him." "She didn't tell anyone about the physical abuse for a long time, so how do we know it was real?"
Some people would judge me; some would doubt me; some
would have my back. But ultimately, this wasn't about me; it
was about the women who wouldn't be abused by him in the
future.

The next day I went to the premiere of the television mini-
series *The Fourth Estate* by Liz Garbus. Because the docuseries
was about the *New York Times*, I was in a room crawling with
reporters, many of whom I knew. I felt the weight of my secret.
I felt the bomb ticking.

Yet another reporter from the *Times* reached out to Robbie
Kaplan directly. Robbie told her she couldn't talk about it. The
reporter then texted her: "Robbie, that thing we discussed the
other night is on my mind. What's eating at me, reportorially,
is that this is the guy charged with investigating [New York
County district attorney Cyrus] Vance (not to mention so many
others). If there's a problematic pattern there, it's got to be publicly documented. Is the issue that the women are reluctant to
see this reported?"

I wrote to Robbie, "We have it under control with two of the most trusted journalists in the world."

The next morning, while I was in a meeting, my phone rang. The screen showed the name of a friend who worked at the *Times*, so I answered.

I said, "I'm in a meeting. Can I call you back in about an hour?"

The voice said, "I think you think I'm someone else."

"Who is this?"

"It's X."

She was the same reporter who had reached out to Robbie.

I told her I was in a meeting.

She asked, "Is there a time that's good for—?" I hung up before she could finish the question.

She tried me repeatedly during the day. I blocked her number.

She then sent me an email: "I'd love to chat with you about some of your women's rights activism, when you have a few minutes."

I thought, "Well, that's hilarious."

I forwarded the email to Jane Mayer, who wrote, "They now have your name and are coming up with a bogus excuse to try to pull you in."

The next day, a friend texted that the *Times* reporter had reached out to her, wanting to talk about me. She tried to call another friend four times; yet another friend said she had called his office and then his cell. It seemed almost random whom the reporter was contacting. Maybe she was going through my website and contacting people mentioned on it? I alerted those who had any knowledge about what I was dealing with to ignore her and block her number.

One friend called, sounding worried. "Are you in danger?"

I said, "I'll be okay."

The reporter didn't seem to understand victims and trauma. You don't lie to or stalk a victim.

A few days later, I spoke with Mayer. She had gotten an email from Eric's PR guy and spoken with him. He said he had heard she was asking questions about Eric. He had heard she was working on a Me Too story. He asked her to let him know.

She simply responded, "Yes. I'll let you know if there's a story."

She said to me, wryly, "It's a hot potato."

After I hung up, I worried that Eric would now have time to gather his troops and assemble his surrogates. We had lost the advantage of surprise.

I thought, "I'm a nobody. He and his people will try to crush me."

I became more scared. I had worked so hard to keep my story airtight, but one whisper had become a thousand. That weekend, Carrie Mae Weems stayed with me.

We talked about how Eric was doing important work as the attorney general, and she asked, "Is this a good time to expose him?"

I responded, "It is, Carrie."

She said, "Are you sure?"

"I've got to do this not just for me. I have to do this for other women."

She said, "Our place in the world is that we should be attractive to men. And we stay silent."

I asked, "Am I doing the right thing?"

She responded, "Yes, unfortunately."

David Remnick gave me a heads-up that a fact-checker would be calling me and that the story would be coming out soon. I had made plans to leave the country on May 9, but he couldn't guarantee that it would not run until after I left. We talked about how it had been a roller coaster. I told him I was scared, shaking all the time, though nobody could tell. I was vigilant about hiding my tremors; digging my nails into my palms and counting my breaths helped. He thanked me for my steadfastness, patience, and trust.

That night, I had a dream. I was at One World Trade Center, in the *New Yorker* offices. I was meeting with various people who were prepping for the release of the story. The last I had heard, there were two women on the record, one anonymous and one as background. I was disappointed that more women wouldn't participate. In the dream, a fact-checker from the *New Yorker* called me to say, "Ma'am, be careful as you walk home."

I asked, "Did he deny what was in the story?"

The fact-checker quietly said, "Yes."

"Did he deny that he called me his slave and property?"

"Yes."

"Did he deny that he hit me in bed?"

"Yes."

Then I saw text messages streaming through on my phone. I realized that the story had hit. As I woke up from the dream, my heart was pounding in my ears.

In my waking life, I packed a suitcase, and my friend Julia picked me up and helped me move to my friend Catherine's place, where I would hide out until I could leave the country.

On Monday, May 7, Remnick called to say that the *New*

Yorker was about to contact Eric's office for comment. That meant that Eric would find out I was participating.

Remnick said the story made him feel sick, on the one hand, but confident, on the other. He said, "Do I love publishing things like this? It's necessary."

Mayer forwarded me the responses from Eric's office. He was denying most of the allegations but also claimed that some of the abuse had been consensual.

Remnick told me, "We're off to the races."

THE FALLOUT

A little before 7:00 p.m. on May 7, I received a text from David Remnick: "The story is up."

I was at a benefit dinner hosted by the artist Laurie Anderson and the writer A. M. Homes to support Yaddo, the artists' community in Saratoga Springs, New York. I took Laurie aside and told her that I had to leave. She asked why.

I said, "A story just came out."

"Are you in it?"

"Yes."

She said, "Then you've done what you need to do. Don't go."

I stayed. For the next two hours, my phone blew up with text messages and missed calls from friends. At the dinner, no one knew what was going on. They weren't looking at their phones.

I was there with Julia, so I felt as calm as could be possible. We left a little before the end of the dinner. The streets were quiet. Catherine, with whom I was staying, called to check on me. Her mother, Aggie, was with her and wanted to speak with me. Aggie wanted me to know she was sorry for me. They were finishing up dinner at a restaurant in the Meatpacking District, a few blocks from where we were. Aggie said to come over so she could give me a hug. Julia and I walked over to the restaurant. Even though the news was everywhere, I felt anonymous as I went to their table. Aggie and Catherine hugged me, and then Aggie gave us a ride to Catherine's place. Catherine, Julia, and I sat around the dining table. They were tracking the news. I hadn't even read the story yet.

I heard that many New York politicians were calling for Eric to resign. I felt ambivalent about many of those pronouncements. Most didn't express sympathy for the victims.

A breaking news alert came on my phone. Eric had issued a statement:

In the last several hours, serious allegations, which I strongly contest, have been made against me. While these allegations are unrelated to my professional conduct or the operations of the office, they will effectively prevent me from leading the office's work at this critical time. I therefore resign my office, effective at the close of business on May 8, 2018.

It had been less than three hours since the *New Yorker* story had run. Remnick told me that the outcome was unprecedented. I felt it was a testament to Mayer and Farrow's airtight reporting. The story had landed like a surgical strike.

Eric's ex-wife issued a statement:

I've known Eric for nearly thirty-five years as a husband, father, and friend. These allegations are completely inconsistent with the

man I know, who has always been someone of the highest charac-
ter, outstanding values, and a loving father. I find it impossible
to believe these allegations are true.

When I read that, I thought that she must have known about his problems, based on what I had heard from the previous girl-friend whom I had connected with a few months before.

Robbie emailed to check on me. I called her and said I was with friends, not reading the news.

She said, "Good. You are a hero."

Robbie had always been so matter-of-fact with me that I was surprised and moved by her compliment.

Catherine was receiving calls from mutual friends. I was feeling less shell-shocked and better able to communicate with people beyond her and Julia. We put the callers on speaker-phone. One friend talked about the strange convergence of my story with the Me Too moment. Another was with a group of lawyers in DC who were talking about how the fact that Eric had resigned within a few hours meant that the allegations had to be true. She said he needed to enter rehab and be gone.

I spoke with Jennifer Gonnerman, who said that with a piece not as strong as this one, I could have been left twisting in the wind for months. Really, there was nothing to celebrate. It wasn't as though I was going to have champagne with friends and toast the outcome. But she said it was one of the first times in history when things hadn't gone wrong for the victims.

Cindi Leive texted that I could read the story and not be ashamed. So I finally did. As I read it, I felt as if I were watch-ing a movie of my life.

I started hearing about the backlash, but it all seemed dumb.

On Twitter, a nutjob conspiracy theorist declared me a "Putin plant." I had my computer in front of me and Julia and Catherine by my side. As I read an email that came in, Julia noticed sadness in my expression. I showed her the note. My mother had written: "Now that everything is in the news I am begging you not to go on tv or news and get cheap publicity." Julia and Catherine looked sad on my behalf. I had gotten so used to being blamed by my mother that I had kind of been expecting that reaction. She couldn't put herself into my shoes and see the bigger picture: that I had done the right thing.

Looking back, navigating my mother's reaction was as difficult as navigating the aftermath of coming forward. On the one hand, I understand that she hadn't signed up for what I did. On the other, I wish she had left me alone or expressed sympathy. I felt the sting of her judgment.

That night, I also received a note from a relative, advising me to "avoid saying anything further to anyone," such as going on talk shows. She also wrote that if I did, I "[might] lose the support of some" who believed I was courageous to come forward.

I was in fact receiving dozens of media requests; I was being offered "platforms" by television talk shows. I knew that the bookers and producers were doing their jobs, but I felt that it was not a time to gloat. I had already planned not to do any follow-up press; the story spoke for itself.

Eric had stepped down; women had been warned. An unexpected development was that Barbara Underwood was appointed acting attorney general, the first woman to hold the position. I felt comforted. The journalist Rebecca Traister later wrote, "One day in June 2018, I turned on the television and saw Christiane Amanpour, the woman hired to host Charlie Rose's PBS show, interviewing Barbara Underwood, the woman who replaced Eric Schneiderman as New York's attorney general, about a lawsuit she'd just filed against the Trump Foundation." Visible change was taking place.

With regard to my mother and my relative, I had to forgive them or else I would have made myself sick. People can be scared to speak their truths because family members silence them. But then the news exploded in Sri Lanka; it was on the front page of the major papers, with some articles focusing salaciously on the "brown slave" terminology. Tongues started wagging, and in Sri Lanka, gossip can kill. My mother was affected by the negativity. However, I felt that anyone who was going to judge me was not someone I needed in my life and not someone my mother should have in her life, either.

Meanwhile, I had been receiving an outpouring of support from friends and strangers all over the world, and I did hear from a few family members, especially among my generation, who applauded my courage and offered me refuge.

The next day, I heard from a friend in my apartment building that a reporter had slipped a note under my door and that an FBI agent had tried to open the door before slipping a business card under it with a note saying she'd like to talk to me. But I was sequestered at Catherine's. Catherine told me a story about Philippe Petit, who was famous for having walked a high wire between the former Twin Towers of the World Trade Center. He had talked about the importance of staying balanced in order to live longer. He advised putting on one's socks and shoes while standing up. I tried it and felt wobbly.

I had worried that my career would be impacted by the *New Yorker* piece. But my boss-to-be at a new arts center called to check on me. He said, "We're still on." Planned Parenthood, for which I had already been working, sent flowers.

The jockeying for Eric's job began almost immediately, with New York City public advocate Letitia James and law professor Zephyr Teachout throwing their hats into the ring. They made public statements denouncing Eric. Meanwhile, the story was being spun through angle after angle. Jane Mayer appeared on the radio on WNYC; Ronan Farrow on television on CNN. I stayed in my cocoon at Catherine's place. The story seemed to have blown up assumptions about intimate violence and domestic violence. It provided a teachable moment. Journalists were writing about consent, abuse, and even racial dynamics in intimate partner relationships.

The Cut ran a feature on "Eric Schneiderman and Men Who Excuse Violence as 'Kink.'" It also ran an informative guide, "Here's How Consent and BDSM Role-Play Actually Work." The sex educator cited, Barbara Carrellas, took offense at Eric's defense of his actions: "Role play means two people had a conversation and decided: *I think this sounds really hot, now how can we sensibly play this out.*" She said the slapping described in the *New Yorker* article was "bang-on brute violence." According to Carrellas:

> In BDSM role-play face-slapping is a trigger for a whole lot of people. The trigger level is so high that we really need to get three times consent. People who slap should learn how to do it safely, and you would never slap someone on an ear. Before the role play, the slapper would ask, are you sure you have no triggers from childhood? Have you ever been slapped before? If so, under what circumstances?

She also said:

It's reported that Schneiderman called one of his partners his "brown slave" and demanded that she repeat that she was his property. Race play is just as, if not more, delicate a negotiation than master-slave. . . . They are not entered into casually. Or when drunk.

Governor Cuomo announced the appointment of a special prosecutor to investigate Eric: Madeline Singas, the Nassau County district attorney, who had a great deal of experience with domestic violence cases. I started to think about what outcome I might want. I had already accomplished my personal goals, but I knew I didn't want to roll back the clock to when people weren't investigated after serious allegations had been aired in the court of public opinion.

For the moment, I put thoughts of the investigation out of my head and boarded a plane to England, where no one would care about the story. I stayed with a cousin in London for a night and then went to visit another cousin and his family in Cambridge. On the train, I read *Writing a Woman's Life*, by Carolyn Heilbrun, in which she captured, among other things, the difficulties women historically faced in speaking their truths. They conformed to the vision to which men and society confined them.

I paused while reading Heilbrun's book to look out the window and gaze at the lush English countryside. I felt safe. After I arrived in Cambridge, I played with my twin nieces. That night my cousin and I watched *Battle of the Sexes*, the one movie we could find that neither of us had seen and both of us were interested in. Set in 1973, it was about the epic tennis match between Billie Jean King and Bobby Riggs—which King had won.

The next morning, I walked around Cambridge University. I stopped in a fudge store. As I bought myself a piece of salted caramel, I thought about how Eric hadn't wanted me to eat sweets. I felt so far away. What awaited me when I returned home?

More news related to my story was breaking in the United States. A lawyer, Peter J. Gleason, claimed to have information about Eric's abuse of two other women many years before me, information that had been given to him by Trump's personal lawyer Michael Cohen. Because of the investigations swirling around Cohen, Gleason didn't want to get caught up in the Schneiderman mess. According to the *New York Times*, Gleason said that Mr. Cohen had "told him that if Mr. Trump, who was thinking of running for New York governor at the time, were to be elected, he would help bring to light the women's accusations against Mr. Schneiderman. A deep animus had existed between the two men, prompted by a $40 million civil fraud lawsuit that Mr. Schneiderman filed against Mr. Trump's for-profit educational venture, Trump University, in August 2013."

I spoke with a friend on the phone, and she said I was like the deus ex machina. David Remnick called and asked if I knew anything about the Gleason story. I hadn't a clue.

He said, "It's like a shitty movie."

The next day was Mother's Day. I spoke with my grandmother. She said, "He referred to you as a brown person. You have a beautiful color. You have a beautiful face." I felt sorry that my family was having to deal with the aftermath of the media storm.

My time in London coincided with a friend's wedding. She is Sri Lankan, and I was nervous because I was going to see many people who knew my family. But the event was a joyous, big Sri Lankan wedding. Sri Lankans like to party; they like to dance and sing. I had a ball.

Meanwhile, I was receiving a stream of notes of support:

On behalf of all Asian women who have been marginalized in relationships of any kind with White men, I thank you for speaking out against AG Schneiderman.

As a survivor, I have some sense of how insane and surreal the experience is.

I've too found myself in relationships being treated in a way that was demeaning and offended my feminist sensibilities, but yet continued on.

I woke up this morning with the sad realization that it's totally safe to say that all of us, all women, everywhere, all ages, at one time or another or on several occasions or on a regular basis, have experienced assault and abuse of some kind from at least one man. But you are also healing us, and inspiring us to speak out and to help educate our daughters and girls and our sons and boys (omg who need so much help!) about boundaries, and respect, and love for one another so that we can all work to eventually turn this thing around.

I was also surprised to receive notes from ex-boyfriends and even my ex-husband, whom I hadn't been in contact with for years. He sent this text:

Hey, I'm sorry for what you are going through, and my heart goes out to you. Sending much strength and love. As you can guess, journalists have started reaching out to me. . . . Other than expressing my support I'm not commenting (obviously). Wishing you greatest strength. As ever I admire your willingness to take a stand and be strong. The world is better for it.

Later, I sent an email to friends: "Your notes of support have sustained me over the last week. I am sorry not to respond to each note individually. Thank you for having my back, offering me a place to hide out, asking me what I need. Knowing you are out there sending good vibes means the world to me."

On my last day in London, I was having brunch at the hotel where I was staying. A little after noon, I heard cheers from upstairs. Breaking news alerts on my phone announced that Prince Harry and Meghan Markle had said "I do." I had forgotten that the royal wedding was happening. I decided to watch the rest of the festivities. When I was young, I had dreamed that I might one day marry a prince.

Before I returned to the United States, I decided to continue to stay away from New York. The story was still exploding, and I had a few weeks before beginning my new job. Julia, who had been with me when the story broke, invited me to join her in Tulum, Mexico, where she was writing a book. I seized the opportunity and booked a frequent-flyer ticket.

I was happy to be in Mexico for many reasons: I was far away from the news in New York. I was also in a place that I felt Americans needed to support; the Trump administration had gone out of its way to villainize Mexico and its people.

The day after I returned home, I produced a shoot at the Museum of Modern Art. It was May 31, about three weeks since my story had become public. I was nervous to be in a room for the first time with people who could connect me in person with the Schneiderman story. But a woman came up to me, held my hand, and said, "There's a lot of love for you in this room. We owe you."

I heard from a friend at the *New York Times* that attempts were ongoing to discredit the story. Eric's ex-wife was working behind the scenes, sending emails to people at the paper. She claimed that the *New Yorker* story was a "witch hunt" and that the magazine wasn't interested in hearing the other side. I told my friend that the *New Yorker* had taken great care in investigating the story and there were even more women with similar stories who were too scared to have their experiences included.

During lunch with a friend, he mentioned that I'd made it onto *The Daily Show*. I hadn't watched the clip, and when I finally did that night, I was terribly disappointed. I sent the show's host, Trevor Noah, the following note:

Dear Mr. Noah:

First, I would like to express my admiration for you. Your humor and brilliance provide much levity and comfort to people like me.

It is because of this that I was saddened and disappointed

by the way my image, name, and color were used in your May 8 episode in connection with the Eric Schneiderman story.

"If he wanted to role-play with a slave, why didn't he cast a black woman? Do you know how hard it is for us to get roles?"

With this statement on your show, you added insult to injury, and re-victimized me. The way in which my situation was described also felt oblivious to the fact that many brown people have in fact been enslaved and discriminated against for centuries, especially in the former colonies, and continue to be, especially in the Middle East.

This is not to equate the history of brown people with that of black people, especially in America. But I want to point out that people of color in different groups have suffered injustice. Post-independence, my people in Sri Lanka endured a long and brutal civil war based on ethnic conflict.

There have been many salacious reports since Jane Mayer and Ronan Farrow's story broke, but this is the only note that I am sending to voice a concern, and that is because I still admire you and hope that you understand.

All best,

Tanya

A few weeks later, I received an apology from a producer of the show.

For the most part, I ignored other negative chatter. Avoiding Facebook and Twitter made it easy.

The investigation by Nassau County DA Madeline Singas began. I met with Singas and her team at Robbie Kaplan's office. I remember being asked, "What evidence of abuse do you have?"

I responded, "I don't have photographs. My face would turn red when he slapped me. But he didn't hit me to bruise me."

I thought, as I had before, "Do I need to have been bruised to be believed?"

I also thought, "I have my memory, which is sharp. There are the stories of at least three other women that are clearly similar to mine. I have a number of friends whom I told along the way, first about his controlling behavior and drinking, then about the slapping, spitting, and verbal abuse."

Singas said that as an investigator, she found it frustrating how high the bar was set for Eric's actions to be considered a crime. She also said, "He fooled a lot of people."

Later that summer, Samantha Bee spoke with Rebecca Traister about her experience with the Schneiderman story.

Rebecca Traister: I was hoping you could tell the story of what the hell happened on the night that it was reported that New York's attorney general had beaten women, and somehow it rebounded negatively to *Full Frontal*.

Samantha Bee: Well, we had done a piece about Schneiderman, I feel like it was seven or eight months ago, in which we characterized him as a superhero. And we owned that because he really was doing just an incredible job of bringing all the AGs together, and he was putting up such great resistance, and . . .

And it rhymes with Spider-Man. So we made all these animations of him, like leaping from tall buildings, and it was a really funny piece. It was really fun to do. I had never met him before. We sat there, we talked for about two or three hours, and that was pretty much it, and we built this piece around him. And then that just quietly existed. And then the day that the piece dropped, and I recall it dropping at 6:47 p.m., because I looked at my watch, and I was like, "I saw the headline." I was making dinner, I saw the headline and was like, "No." And then I read the article really fast. It was just horrifying. We learned that he had tweeted at the show that day, Eric Schneiderman had, with the animations of himself. And he was like, "Remember when I was on *Full* . . . ?" He literally clung to us like we were his feminist life raft.

Toward the end of the summer, I decided to visit my mother in Los Angeles. After I arrived, while I was in my bedroom working on my computer, my mother stood in the doorway and asked, "That jerk has not contacted you?"

I said, "He's unheard of." I meant that I hadn't heard from him.

"I'm not your enemy, Tanya. Don't think your friends are more important than me."

I didn't consider her my enemy. I admired what she had done to keep our family together despite the abuse she herself had dealt with. I felt sorry for her.

She asked, "Are you seeing a psychiatrist?"

I replied, "Yes, for years."

"Sometimes they mess you up," she said. Then she added, "Just say three Hail Marys. That's more than enough. Sometimes psychiatrists put thoughts in your head." She said that if I prayed, I wouldn't be like this.

I said, "My entire life you have made me feel bad about myself."

That ended the conversation. Why did our conversations often have to be so difficult? I worried that I wasn't the person she wanted me to be, but I felt that I was doing the best that I could.

While I was at her home, she wanted me to sort through old boxes. As I sat in the garage, going through box after box, I felt overwhelmed. As much as I wanted to keep moving forward and moving on, I realized I had been through a lot—a long stretch of facing death, divorce, and then abuse. I have an aversion to self-pity. I come from a country where people have suffered immeasurable loss from wars, imperialism, and natural disasters; I have nothing to complain about. This principle has served me well in hard situations, to keep going and never give up. But it has also resulted in my tolerating more than I should. I see now how it affected my putting up with Eric's treatment until I got help.

In that moment in the garage, I had to take a break from arranging my things, sit down, and cry.

After Los Angeles, I went to Portland, where I had first started the journey of coming forward. It was raining lightly when I arrived. As soon as the sun came out, I took a hike. I walked by the house that looked like a dream catcher. The air smelled so green. There was no pollution. I went down a set of stairs onto a trail. Sometimes I closed my eyes and could see a scene from my life with him. It felt far away and unreal.

I thought, "What would happen if I fell into a ravine?" It might be the right way to leave this life, lost in nature. As I exited the trail, I heard the Beatles' "Here Comes the Sun" playing loudly in a car.

Back in New York, I was in the *Glamour* office to make Women of the Year videos. One morning, I felt fragile. There was a clenching in my chest, a shuddering that rippled through my body. I biked from my apartment along the East River. As I approached Fulton Street, a Chinese woman on a bike raised her hand up high and waved at me. I didn't know her. I wondered if there was something wrong.

Loudly, she said, "Good morning!"

That was the unexpected moment I needed.

After I docked my bike, I was walking toward the World Trade Center when a voice gently said, "Excuse me." I turned around. The woman asked, "Do you know where Broadway is?" We were on Church Street. She was a block away. I pointed her in the right direction. Then she said, "One-twenty Broadway."

My heart dropped. She was looking for the building where Eric's office used to be.

In the months after the *New Yorker* piece appeared, I managed to do some public engagements. I spoke at two panels at the Aspen Ideas Festival, one on freedom of expression, the other on the work of Carrie Mae Weems. While there, I attended a number of Me Too–related panels. Each time, I wondered if people knew my story.

A few months later, I was asked to be on a Brooklyn Book Festival panel on "The Art of the Accused"—how we view art by those who have been exposed as predators. I told the organizer that I was worried about stalkers. I also said I was worried about being cornered with questions about my personal situation. She said they would have extra security and that the questions would be submitted on note cards.

A. O. Scott, the film critic at the *New York Times*, was on the panel. He had written about Woody Allen in the context of Me Too. I thought about how Eric loved Woody Allen movies, which made me cringe. I had stopped watching Woody Allen movies after Allen had started sleeping with his longtime partner Mia Farrow's adopted daughter, Soon-Yi Previn, whom he later married.

On the panel, I said that we had a perpetrator on the Supreme Court, not knowing that hours later we would learn that with the nomination of Brett Kavanaugh, we would soon have another perpetrator on the Supreme Court.

Back at my apartment building, I bumped into a neighbor.

He said, "We haven't seen you in a while. We wanted to say sorry for what happened. And we support you."

I said, "Thank you."

"I hope it's okay that I'm saying something."

"Yes, it's human. Thank you."

I continued to stay in touch with Jane Mayer and Ronan Farrow. They wanted to do a follow-up story about Eric, especially when the results of Singas's investigation were announced. They now had more women who wanted to share their stories about Eric. Farrow told me he was working on a big story; he'd have to do press for a few weeks, and then he could turn his attention to the follow-up.

That big story was about CBS chairman and CEO Les Moonves and the women whose careers had fallen apart because of their devastating encounters with him. Farrow's piece broke while I was with a friend on a train heading upstate. She and I sat across from each other, reading the article and giving each other horror-stricken glances. I felt triggered. I felt empathy for the victims and recalled memories of my own experience. I recognized that that triggering would be with me for a long time, maybe for the rest of my life.

When we reached the house we had rented, we were joined by two friends. The Moonves story was all we could talk about. One friend had worked for him. We realized that all of us had been close to or victims of predators in the workplace, which showed how pervasive the problem was. We talked about how perpetrators get away with it; they always do. That's why it keeps happening—when they get big payouts, when their friends don't hold them accountable, they experience no consequences.

I decided to do a deep dive into the coverage around my story. I watched Jane Mayer on MSNBC, criminal defense lawyer Rikki Klieman on CBS, CBS This Morning cohost Gayle King's disgust with Eric calling me a "brown slave." I was fascinated and also saddened. Indeed, my name and image had been everywhere. In most instances, the news outlets had dug up old photos from the internet. I felt bad for the people who were in the photos with me. I wondered if they had received phone calls. I wondered if I should apologize to them.

But my presence in the news cycle had passed, and my life had gone on. Moreover, I had learned a lot about how to deal with abuse, how to come forward—and why the laws covering intimate partner violence need to change.

THE LESSON

While I was working on this chapter, I went to see Heidi Schreck's Broadway show *What the Constitution Means to Me*. I wasn't prepared for how much the play was about the history of violence against women. Schreck explores the legacy of trauma passed down from generation to generation among the women in her family and sets it against the backdrop of the institutionalized inequality of women in the United States. She talks about her guilt over being of the first generation in her family not to experience violence. She talks about the failure of this country to ratify the Equal Rights Amendment and how her mother cried about that failure. At one point, she asks, "When will white women stop betraying women?" She is referring to both implicit and explicit ways in which white women support the patriarchy and suppress a woman's right to choose and to live the life she wants to live.

In 2016, 47 percent of white women voted for Trump. If they hadn't helped him get elected, I believe the seismic reckoning wouldn't have begun. The misogyny, as well as the racism, that he unleashed revealed the wounds America has tried to conceal. As Rebecca Traister wrote, "One year after Donald Trump had faced no repercussions for having admitted to grabbing women nonconsensually, women appeared hell-bent on ensuring that other men *would* be forced—at long last—to accept some consequence."

Joshua Green, in his book *Devil's Bargain: Steve Bannon, Donald Trump, and the Storming of the Presidency*, described his experience with white supremacist and former presidential adviser Steve Bannon while watching the Time's Up action at the Golden Globes. "It's a Cromwell moment!" Bannon had said. "It's even more powerful than populism. It's deeper. It's primal. It's elemental. The long black dresses and all that—this is the Puritans. It's anti-patriarchy. . . . You watch. The time has come. Women are gonna take charge of society."

Bannon had in part orchestrated the successful manipulation of Americans through populist tactics that relied on sowing fear and division. Suketu Mehta, the author of *This Land Is Our Land: An Immigrant's Manifesto*, has said, "Populists tell false stories well. We have to tell true stories better."

The cultural critic Elizabeth Méndez Berry told me, with regard to awareness of intimate violence, "So many people have been silent about their experiences for so long. Now that they're talking, it's an avalanche. I do believe in the power of telling our stories, but I also think that without profound changes in how people view women, and what they believe we deserve, we won't transform this society. We need to shift people's worldviews, and particularly those of young men and women, so they can have the beautiful, healthy, pleasurable relationships they deserve."

In the wake of Me Too and Time's Up, we have to look at how we raise our children, how we change the way we condition sexuality in our children, and how our culture has evolved. Jennifer Friedman has spoken with me about the importance of raising boys to be feminists; boys have to go through training about how to treat women and other men with respect and kindness. Girls have to go through training about how to stand up for themselves and how to avoid situations where they might be harassed, abused, and endangered. These situations begin on the playground. As a friend said, "We are taught that if a boy hits you, it means he likes you; if he teases you, he likes you. It starts right there."

Educators, like parents, play a major role in how children learn about gender dynamics, and they should go through training themselves. Numerous positive examples have emerged. For decades, Tony Porter, the author and activist who cofounded A Call to Men, has conducted violence prevention and healthy manhood programs around the world. Andrew Reiner, in his *New York Times* article "Boy Talk: Breaking Masculine Stereotypes," discussed training programs for boys "about the ways to recognize and prevent sexual and gendered violence" and to help them navigate relationships in the Me Too era. He mentioned a weekly lunch-time boys' group at the Sheridan School, a K–8 private school in northwest Washington, DC, and a program called Becoming a Man (BAM) for high school students on Chicago's South Side. As the professor and activist Brittney Cooper wrote, "In every part of their lives, young men need access to conversations about what it means to be a man in ways that are not rooted in power, dominance, and violence." Those conversations need to continue when the young men become adults.

But how can any of us feel truly protected if our government doesn't seem to care about the treatment of women? As the survivors' advocate Rachna Khare pointed out to me, "The White House [under Trump] quietly changed the definition of domestic violence to only include harms that constitute a felony or misdemeanor crime. This would ignore psychological, emotional, financial, and verbal abuse and control. I'm worried that we're going backward and that we need bipartisan leadership to merely get us back to where we used to be."

By contrast, Joe Biden, while a senator, wrote the Violence Against Women Act (VAWA), which included setting up a national hotline and funding shelters and crisis centers. During his 2020 presidential campaign, Biden pledged to enhance and reauthorize VAWA.

While Trump was in office, I saw a young performance artist do a show about male fragility. She talked about how she had learned what it was like to live in a time when "the biggest gaslighting, abusive boyfriend you've ever had is president." About being an activist, she said, "We can take a break when we don't live in a misogynist dystopia."

The stream of perpetrators being outed could be endless. What's important, however, is not to fixate on individual cases but to focus on eradicating the mindset that encourages harmful behavior. It's going to take a long time, but I think we can get to a safer world, and I find hope in this statistic: an October 2018 article in the *New York Times* stated that at the time, more than two hundred prominent men had "lost their jobs after public allegations of sexual harassment. . . . Forty-three percent of their replacements were women. Of those, one-third are in news media, one-quarter in government, and one-fifth in entertainment and the arts."

Catharine MacKinnon, in the *Atlantic*, wrote:

The world's first mass movement against sexual abuse, #MeToo took off from the law of sexual harassment, quickly overtook it, and is shifting cultures everywhere, electrifyingly demonstrating butterfly politics in action. The early openings of the butterflies' wings were the legal, political, and conceptual innovations of the 1970s, but it is the collective social intervention of the #MeToo movement that is setting off the cataclysmic transformations of which a political butterfly effect is capable.

In an interview with Poppy Harlow of CNN, Supreme Court justice Ruth Bader Ginsburg had said she believed that the Me Too movement "will have 'staying power' and that she doesn't worry about a serious backlash." She had noted, "It's amazing that for the first time, women are really listened to because sexual harassment had often been dismissed as 'well, she made it up.'" Ginsburg has long been a beacon for me, even more so since her death.

Another beacon for me has been Anita Hill. I was in college when the Clarence Thomas confirmation hearings were taking place. In a 2018 feature in *New York* magazine about women and power, Hill said, "Everyone likes to remind me that I did not win. I like to say I won, because I shared my story and people became much more aware of a problem that has been plaguing all of us."

In a May 9, 2019, op-ed for the *New York Times*, Hill described the devastating effect of the hearings: "If the Senate Judiciary Committee, led then by Mr. Biden, had done its job and held a

hearing that showed that its members understood the serious-
ness of sexual harassment and other forms of sexual violence, the
cultural shift we saw in 2017 after #MeToo might have begun in
1991—with the support of the government. . . . Sexual violence
is a national crisis that requires a national solution. . . . This crisis
calls for all leaders to step up and say: 'The healing from sexual
violence must begin now. I will take up that challenge.'"

The Senate Judiciary Committee suppressed reports by other
women about Thomas and blocked the testimony of women
such as Sukari Hardnett, who, like Hill, had worked under
Thomas at the Equal Employment Opportunity Commission.
Hill was forced to take the hit on her own. Biden would later
acknowledge the failure of the committee and himself back
then, and Hill endorsed him for president in 2020. But that
committee in 1991 did irreparable damage by putting a sexual
predator onto the Supreme Court.

In 2018, when the Senate confirmed Brett Kavanaugh as
a Supreme Court justice despite credible allegations of sexual assault by him from several women, Dr. Christine Blasey
Ford in particular, history repeated itself. Kavanaugh's denials
verged on the lunatic. As Jane Mayer remarked in an interview
by Molly Langmuir for *Elle*, "Almost everybody was a jerk in
high school in some way, right? For me, what was much more
important was how he deals with the truth about who he was.
And the fact that he couldn't means you've got somebody on
the court who, I think almost certainly, lied under oath."

I vividly recall the day of Dr. Ford's testimony. I happened to
be in Washington, DC, for meetings at Planned Parenthood.
Everyone in the office seemed shaken up, and I was especially
affected by the sight of young women crying. In Dr. Ford's

written and verbal testimony, she said, "I am here today not because I want to be. I am terrified. I am here because I believe it is my civic duty to tell you what happened to me while Brett Kavanaugh and I were in high school." She continued, "Brett put his hand over my mouth to stop me from screaming. This was what terrified me the most, and has had the most lasting impact on my life. It was hard for me to breathe, and I thought that Brett was accidentally going to kill me."

Similar to what had happened with the Thomas hearings, many women did not get to tell their stories about Kavanaugh. And both Jane Mayer and Ronan Farrow said that there were other women who were too scared to come forward. Kavanaugh's confirmation was a fait accompli.

What might happen if we reach a majority in Congress that actually believes in truth over party loyalty? Might Thomas and Kavanaugh be impeached? A 2017 *Time*/SurveyMonkey poll "found that Republicans were significantly more likely to excuse sexual misdeeds in their own party. The survey found that whereas a majority of Republicans and Democrats agree that a Democratic Congressman accused of sexual harassment should resign (71% and 74% respectively), when the accused offender was in the GOP, only 54% of Republicans would demand a resignation (compared to 82% of Democrats)."

Nonetheless, there have been positive steps on both sides of the political aisle. Congress passed rules mandating sexual harassment training in both branches. After allegations about US Appeals Court judge Alex Kozinski became public, Supreme Court chief justice John Roberts "called for a special working group to examine procedures for employee complaints." Outside of government, the Academy of Motion Picture Arts and Sciences issued a new code of conduct. Dawn Hudson, its CEO, said in a statement, "There is no place in the Academy for people who abuse their status, power or influence in a manner that violates recognized standards of decency."

To break the inextricable link between misogyny and power, there must be graver repercussions for perpetrators. People waste time asking "How could So-and-So do that?" or "How can they live with themselves?" Although perpetrators such as Bill O'Reilly and Les Moonves have been shamed, their money has bought them impunity. Take their money away. Stop the golden parachutes. There must also be reparations for victims. Make the perpetrators pay for their victims' legal and therapy bills. Make them pay for every year their victims have to deal with the trauma after the abuse. In addition, scrutinize and publicize the investment portfolios and charitable donations of perpetrators.

After Eric Schneiderman resigned, millions of dollars remained in his campaign fund—hundreds of thousands of dollars of which he used to pay his legal bills. A few friends who had contributed to his campaign were eager to get their money back. After one of them figured out how to request the refund, she sent me the email address to contact. In February 2019, I wrote to it:

> I hope you are well.
>   After much deliberation, I am writing to request the return of my donation to the Schneiderman campaign.
>   I will re-donate that amount to a worthy cause.
>   Thank you for your attention.
>
>   Sincerely,
>   Tanya

I received a response and then a check for my $750. It felt incredibly ironic that my donation, albeit relatively small, had been part of a pot that he was using to cover his legal expenses.

Eric also turned his campaign fund into his private philanthropic foundation; I heard that he reached out to organizations to offer large sums of money. A source told me that the head of one organization was reluctant to accept the donation out of concern that it would be used to redeem Eric. Meanwhile, another organization that focuses on girls and gender-based violence accepted $1.5 million. That made me sad. On the one hand, it could put the money to good use. On the other, I agreed with a friend who said that the organization had accepted blood money. My opinion is that the funds should have been offered back to the original donors, so they could redistribute the money to organizations of their choosing. It shouldn't be up to Eric to decide where that money goes.

Meanwhile, the bar is set too high for perpetrators to be charged with a crime. I do believe in redemption; I believe in restorative justice. If a perpetrator has acknowledged his crime and/or done time, perhaps we can be open. But most perpetrators have not done either.

Typically, perpetrators don't face serious financial or legal consequences. Like Eric Schneiderman, they often deny the allegations, even when they are investigated and corroborated. In some instances, perpetrators have the gall to see themselves as victims. Russell Simmons, for one, posted #NotMe when he was exposed by the actress and screenwriter Jenny Lumet's horrific account of being assaulted by him. They seem to think that they're good guys and the women merely misinterpreted their actions. And many miss the limelight.

Not long after numerous allegations came out about Tavis Smiley and his PBS show was canceled, he went on the road with an "inspirational" series called *The Upside with Tavis Smiley* and a five-city "town hall" tour to talk about relationships in the workplace. The accused journalist John Hockenberry wrote a "poor me" piece for *Harper's*; and Matt Lauer wrote one for Mediaite. Those outlets made the disastrous decision to give platforms to the accused when they could have given platforms to their victims.

In many instances, perpetrators have attempted to wash their dirty laundry with philanthropy, as in the case of Ron Burkle hosting benefits for rape crisis centers and Harvey Weinstein supporting Planned Parenthood. Jeffrey Epstein called himself a "renowned educational investor." In 2012, he undertook "a public relations campaign to counter bad press about his sexual exploits"—which included abusing and trafficking dozens of underage girls—and donated "millions to scientific research."

Weinstein was finally arrested, tried, and sent to prison. Epstein was also arrested but committed suicide before he could be tried. But what about their enablers? In the case of Epstein, his accomplice, Ghislaine Maxwell, was eventually arrested. I don't even try to wrap my head around the psychology of these women who facilitate the depravity of these men, except to consider that they enjoyed the conduit to power these men provided for them.

Perpetrators and their enablers harbor each other even after they've been exposed. During the 2019 Sundance Film Festival, David Glasser, the former president and chief operating officer for the Weinstein Company, announced that he was starting a new production company with the backing of . . . Ron Burkle. Meanwhile, the filmmaker John Lasseter, after being dumped by Pixar for his inappropriate behavior toward women and his creation of a fratlike atmosphere, went on to be hired by Sky-dance Media, a production company under Paramount Animation. Female employees were told that they could choose to decline to work with him. The actress Emma Thompson took a stand and pulled out of a Skydance project with a pointed letter: "It feels very odd to me that you and your company would consider hiring someone with Mr. Lasseter's pattern of misconduct given the present climate in which people with the kind of power that you have can reasonably be expected to step up to the plate."

Perpetrators have to suffer tangible consequences, yet the law often lets them get away with their crimes. Inadequate legal frameworks, including the US Constitution, need to be updated. As Ginia Bellafante of the *New York Times* pointed out about New York State's laws:

> *Felony assault in New York State requires the demonstration of significant injury—a broken limb, a gunshot wound, serious impact to an organ. If none of these can be proved, a prosecutor might then move on to consider misdemeanor assault, and here, too, she might run into trouble. . . . a prosecutor would have to prove that there was intent to cause physical injury.*

Moreover, the United States has not ratified the Equal Rights Amendment. The late, great Justice Ginsburg had said, "Equal stature of men and women is as fundamental as the basic human rights. . . . every Constitution in the world written since the year 1950 has the equivalent statement that men and women are people of equal citizenship stature." Catharine MacKinnon wrote that "the only legal change in US law that matches the [Me Too] movement's scale would be the passage of an Equal Rights Amendment. . . . It could renovate interpretations of equality in a more substantive and intersectional direction, reconfiguring the concept by guaranteeing sex equality for all under the Constitution for once."

A World Health Organization paper on violence by intimate partners highlighted the importance and success of treatment programs for perpetrators. According to research from the United States, the majority of men in treatment programs "remain physically non-violent for up to 2 years, with lower rates for longer follow-up periods." But there was a high dropout rate of between one-third and one-half of men who enrolled in the programs, and many who were referred never enrolled. The paper cited the need for accountability through criminal justice measures. Pittsburgh, Pennsylvania, for example, "began issuing arrest warrants for men who failed to appear at the programme's initial interview session." As a result, its nonattendance rate "dropped from 36% to 6% between 1994 and 1997."

In addition to strengthening laws and centering victims in policy making, we must improve reporting and monitoring mechanisms. Power systems lend themselves to corruption and abuse. Monitoring has to happen outside the system. And the reporting process has to be less cumbersome and intimidating; "human resources" too often means "corporate resources."

I am reminded of the case of Brock Turner, who in 2015, while a student at Stanford University, assaulted an unconscious woman by a dumpster. He ended up serving only three months of the already paltry six-month sentence he received. His father said that Turner shouldn't suffer for "20 minutes of action," meaning the time during which his son had assaulted the woman. What his father and many others don't understand is that whether the abuse lasts twenty minutes, a day, a month, a year, or decades, the scars of being harassed, assaulted, raped, and brutalized leave an indelible impact. Moments of abuse mark time before and after. As the media critic Soraya Chemaly wrote, "Men learn to regard rape as a moment in time; a discreet [*sic*] episode with a beginning, middle, and end. But for women, rape is thousands of moments that we fold into ourselves over a lifetime."

Brock Turner's survivor read a letter at his trial:

> [T]o girls everywhere, I am with you. . . . As the author Anne Lamott once wrote, "Lighthouses don't go running all over an island looking for boats to save; they just stand there shining." Although I can't save every boat, I hope that by speaking today, you absorbed a small amount of light.

At the time, she was anonymous, but years later, Chanel Miller told her story through a memoir titled *Know My Name: A Memoir*. In 2016, the letter she had read at the trial was viewed more than 11 million times in four days; in 2019, her book went on to win the National Book Critics Circle Award for Autobiography and numerous other awards.

We can turn rage into light by advocating for change at the local and national levels. We can start by asking our representatives where they stand with regard to protections for victims and accountability for perpetrators and enablers. We can support candidates who have the courage to build the safer world we envision for ourselves. We have to let go of the old ways of power that have oppressed and silenced women.

MOVING FORWARD

During a phone call with my grandma, she asked how I was doing.

"I'm all right."

She said, "Give him a kick in the ass. You do it. He deserves it. I'm glad you got rid of him. Grandma is always there for you."

My grandma always tells it like it is. But in this instance, I didn't have to do anything except get on with my life and recover. The investigation of Eric was ongoing. I had supported it by speaking with the team led by Nassau County DA Madeline Singas. I was patient with the process. Eventually there would be an outcome.

In the summer of 2018, I went to my high school reunion, where I found myself often observing rather than engaging. I wanted to hang back. It had not been long since my story had become public; many people thanked me for coming forward. One friend said she hadn't expected to see me there. I was happy to be around people who had known me for a long time.

On the ride home, I commented to my closest friend from school, Gabriela, that Massachusetts was an emotional state for me. It was where I had gone to high school, college, and graduate school. I had lived there when I was married. She reminded me that it was also where I had had my surgeries, at Massachusetts General Hospital.

The day after the *New Yorker* story came out, a *New York Times* editor reached out asking if I would write an op-ed. I wrote her back, "My plan for when the article broke was to let the story speak for itself and not enter the media frenzy. So, I've been hiding." But she and I continued to stay in touch over the next few months. After Dr. Ford's testimony at the Kavanaugh hearings, I felt I was ready for an op-ed to come out. I was hopeful that I could provide a window into the process of coming forward and the trauma that never goes away.

On October 5, the *Times* editor gave me a heads-up that the piece would come out that weekend. To be safe, I moved out of my apartment and into Catherine's home again. I sent a note to my mother, brother, and sister-in-law to alert them, adding "Maybe don't read it. But if you do, I hope it doesn't cause concern. I am absolutely doing great and feel I did the right thing." To my mother, I added, "Please don't be mad."

The piece ran on the evening of October 6, a few hours after Brett Kavanaugh was confirmed to the Supreme Court. Here is an excerpt:

Ultimately, I take responsibility for staying, but doing so took a deep toll. . . . I didn't understand until after the relationship ended how physiological the impact is—the shaking and shuddering that happens suddenly, when I feel trapped, when I feel mocked. Symptoms of post-traumatic stress are a real and common reaction to abuse. Sometimes when I look in the mirror, I hear his voice in my head belittling me. Still, while I regret getting into the relationship, I don't regret coming forward. . . .

[W]e've learned this past year that our words can chip away at violence, and can challenge the way society conditions us to accept it. Recently, I have been reading Naomi Alderman's novel "The Power," about a future society in which women discover hidden physical abilities, which includes this passage: "A dozen women turned into a hundred. A hundred turned into a thousand. The police retreated. The women shouted; some made placards. They understood their strength, all at once."

We've learned that we are not alone. We understand our strength, all at once.

I received many notes, including from my mother, who wrote, "I am only sad that you had to go through all this. You are strong just like your mother. I am not mad. Remember no one loves you more. I love you so much and will always support you. Next time if you find someone let me know, and I will give you my opinion." After reading this, I felt an opening, a healing, a move toward a positive place between my mother and myself. I thought, "I had tried so hard time and time again to do the right thing. I am sorry I had kept failing her. But I had tried. I really had." I felt that she and I just have to forgive each other.

I was also touched by this note from Rachna Khare, who is cited elsewhere in this book:

Your story shook me to my core. I wanted to say thank you. Thank you for so poignantly describing the elation of love, the cycle of manipulation, and the pain of violence. It's difficult, especially in the South Asian culture, to talk about sex—even in a positive context. You pulled back the curtain not only on sexual violence, but on the nuances that we, as women of color, specifically experience.

In my work, I often find it hard to tell stories of South Asian survivors. Like all women, our identities are complex and, therefore, our experiences are multilayered. We could peel back for eternities and there would still be layers left. Your account was gripping—it was painful and also hopeful, it was compassionate but not sanitized. It was educational and also poetic, it was your truth and yet so incredibly relatable to us all. In less than 2,000 words, you captured the intersectionality, complexity, and truth of sexual violence.

We sent your piece to our clients who we are able to contact safely. A copy sits in our lobby and in our counseling offices. I want to thank you for sharing your truth and for making us feel less alone because, as you said, we can now "understand our strength all at once."

In the op-ed, I wrote about being nervous about engaging in an intimate relationship again. That fear was acute. What if a man hit me? What if I stopped him and he told me he needed to do it to get aroused? Fortunately, I was introduced to a man who treated me so well that I felt like crying. We first met in early 2018, but I was keeping a big secret then and was nowhere near ready for a relationship. Months later, after the *New Yorker* story broke, he wrote out of the blue to check on me. I was surprised. And he continued to reach out, until eventually we met in person.

We spent a few nights together. He didn't criticize my scars, my breasts. He did not make me feel less than. He made me feel good about myself. As we drove through a canyon to a restaurant one night, an enormous owl standing on the road looked at us and flew away. Superstition dictates that an owl crossing one's path can be a warning. It could mean that some-one is going to die. But the owl also represents Athena, the goddess of wisdom and strategy. An owl sat beside Athena so she could see the truth. An owl guarded the Acropolis. I love owls, the way they turn their heads all around. At my place in Portland, an owl has occasionally perched on my deck and looked at me with big eyes.

Portland is where I first wrote my first-person narrative and made the decision to come forward. A year later, I went back there to work on this book. I printed out hundreds of pages of notes and research. After about a week, I felt I was ready to review the material. I was in a good place. But the notes I had recorded at the time of the abuse now cut like a knife. I felt pain acutely in my gut. It was a sinking feeling. It was a caving-in feeling. It felt as though my heart were burning down. It felt like hopelessness.

It wasn't just my story. It was all the stories that people had shared with me and that I had researched. I thought, "The problem will never be solved. As long as there are the con-structs of money and real estate, there will be power dynamics that give rise to abuse. It doesn't matter how many laws or law enforcement officers are put in place to monitor and protect. The laws will be broken; predators will get away with it; enablers will protect them; victims will suffer."

I told no one about my depression for a few weeks. I felt as though I was spiraling. I started making plans for how to leave this world. When I had had my surgeries in 2012, the hospital staff had suggested that I write a will, authorize a proxy to make medical decisions on my behalf, and leave a list of instructions. I had put documents into an envelope that I had left in my desk drawer with the words "In case of untimely death" on it. Now would I deal with the logistics of dying?

I thought of the ways: a knife, a sheet, a belt—not pills (where would I get them?), not a plunge into the hills near my house (I might be eaten by animals). Thoughts of people I knew who had attempted to kill themselves or succeeded in doing so swirled through my mind. But when the thoughts paused, I realized that either I was here or I wasn't, and I knew I had to reach out. I emailed a handful of friends that I was feeling very low and that the last two years had finally caught up with me. They rallied around me. Through their calls and notes, they helped me look out and up. I loved my friends and didn't want to never see them again. Also, I knew that somehow one day, if I worked really hard, my story could help others.

I kept writing.

During that low period, I said to my friend Farai, "The bad guys win."

She said, "But the storytellers also win."

I wrote my way out of the darkness.

CODA

November 7, 2018, the night after the midterm elections, Melissa Silverstein took me to the taping of *Full Frontal with Samantha Bee*. At the security check, the guard said that he had to hold on to my pepper spray and I could pick it up after the show. I had been carrying that pepper spray since April. I didn't feel fear anymore, but I continued to keep it in my purse.

Melissa is the founder of the advocacy group Women and Hollywood and of the Athena Film Festival at Barnard College. When the taping was done, the producer and correspondent of *Full Frontal* came over to say hi to her. I felt reticent as the woman approached. We had met when I was making the *Glamour* Women of the Year video about Bee. Would she recognize me? Would she connect me with Eric Schneiderman? But I decided to hold my head up high and thanked her.

That same night, I received a note from Robbie Kaplan, indicating that Madeline Singas was expected to make an announcement the next day about the Schneiderman investigation. Singas wrote, "I believe the women who shared their experiences with our investigation team; however[,] legal impediments, including statutes of limitations, preclude criminal prosecution." She also said that she had proposed a new state law to "protect victims of sexually motivated violence by making it illegal to hit, shove, slap or kick someone without their consent for 'the purpose of sexual arousal or gratification.'"

Eric issued a statement: "I recognize that District Attorney Singas' decision not to prosecute does not mean I have done nothing wrong. I accept full responsibility for my conduct in my relationships with my accusers, and for the impact it had on them." He also said that he had been seeking help in a rehab facility and was "committed to a lifelong path of recovery and making amends to those I have harmed."

I felt that was a positive outcome: a strong statement from the DA, proposed changes in legislation, and Eric's acknowledgment of wrongdoing. All three elements felt validating, but I was surprised by Eric's words. I figured that he'd had no choice but to make that kind of statement and might not actually mean it. But I was glad that he was in rehab. Those developments became part of an extraordinary week, alongside the midterm election results that included Letitia James becoming New York State attorney general, the first female and first African American in that position, and a record number of women running in and, in many cases, winning state and local elections.

At the time of Singas's announcement, I was working again on the *Glamour* Awards. That same day, during the staging session, when my tribute videos were reviewed, the group spontaneously clapped for me. They were applauding the videos, but it felt like an affirmation of what I had done in coming forward.

A woman sitting next to me said suddenly, "I noticed your scar."

She pulled down her sweater to show me the center of her chest. She had a scar, too. We high-fived. She told me she had had a bovine valve implanted. She asked me what mine was for. I told her cancer. I now felt proud of my scars. At the ceremony, I met Judge Rosemarie Aquilina, who had presided over the trial of Larry Nassar, the sports doctor who had sexually abused so many gymnasts.

The following week, I went to Boston for my annual CT scan. In the waiting room, as happened only in that moment every year, it hit me that I felt odd being there; the others were mostly much older. I could feel them looking at me. All of us might have been wondering what the others had had. Every year for at least ten years, from 2012, I'm told, I should have this experience. It marks time.

As I arrived at the train station to return to New York, my phone rang. It was the doctor's office. The nurse asked if I was still in Boston; the radiologist wanted me to come back for more tests. My heart dropped. I had about seventy-five minutes to get to the hospital and back. I doubted I could make it. If I didn't, I would be stuck in Boston for Thanksgiving, because all of the subsequent trains were sold out. But I did make it. The last time I had gotten a call at a train station about returning for a medical test was in 2012, when I would eventually be diagnosed with a GIST and a thymoma. But this time, when the doctor called later with the results, there was no recurrence. This time, I didn't have to stop in my tracks.

I could keep moving until the next round of tests, in a year. I could work on this book.

Getting back to writing, I thought about all the advice that I wished I'd been given and that I wanted to give others who are being victimized. I made a list:

- Document what is happening. Include dates and correlate them with supporting material like email exchanges and photos.
- Tell someone—ideally more than one person—whom you trust not to tell anyone else.
- Figure out whom you can speak with who will know what to do. (In my case, one friend put me in touch with Jennifer Friedman, and another connected me with Robbie Kaplan.)
- Know that you are not alone and you are not crazy.
- It's okay to feel traumatized, but please don't feel ashamed.
- If your partner is not willing to acknowledge the problem *and* get professional help, get away. Your partner is probably not going to change.
- Don't worry about your abuser. Focus on yourself.
- You are the most important part of this equation.

Last, I would tell all women what Elizabeth Méndez Berry had told me: "Put pleasure first: Learn about your own body and how to please yourself on your terms, not somebody else's. Develop a coven of feminist friends who will ride for you and challenge you, lovingly tell you the hard truths when you don't want to hear them."

While I was working on this book, a friend told me that her office was being moved to 120 Broadway, where Eric's office had been. The universe was not only trying to liberate me from a long stretch of personal and health setbacks; it was encouraging me to conquer my fear of certain places and situations.

After the CT scans, when I got home to New York, the place where I had felt trapped before, I felt a leavening. On May 7 of that same year, my story of intimate violence had been revealed to the world. Six months later, I felt free.

EPILOGUE

Out of the blue, in the fall of 2019, I received an email from a previous girlfriend of Eric's whom I had not been aware of before. Her name had not come up during Jane Mayer and Ronan Farrow's reporting. The coda has a coda.

Below is her note. I've left out identifying details.

Dear Tanya,

I hope it's appropriate to reach out.

Eric and I were together in XX—we met at an event held by XX and broke up just after XX. Eric and I did not remain in contact save for running into each other at dharma events.

Eric was abusive. I told no one about the abuse when it was happening because I was ashamed. This also meant that I could not get the help I needed.

Until the *New Yorker* piece, only my husband knew about the abuse. I have since been in counseling and have opened up to friends. I've started to speak out but have never disclosed who hurt me.

I am grateful to you for your clear-seeing and for raising awareness about this disgusting violence. You are helping so many.

I am ready to share my experience if you would find it useful. I would appreciate meeting you.

I searched her name to make sure she was real. She was. I asked my lawyer Robbie Kaplan if I could respond to her. Robbie said, "Of course. And that is lovely."

The woman's cell number was in her email, so I texted her. She responded quickly and asked if I would get together with her. We arranged to meet at One World Trade Center, where I was working again on *Glamour* Women of the Year.

As soon as I met her, I felt she had gentle energy. She had a kind face. I thought, "Eric sure knew how to snag impressive women."

I took her up to the Condé Nast cafeteria. By coincidence, David Remnick was there. Otherwise, the place was mostly empty. It was late afternoon. She and I took a seat near a window, where we could see the Statue of Liberty in the distance.

As she started telling me her story, I reminded myself to keep breathing to stay calm. I was reminded of how I had felt when I had met with the previous girlfriend in LA. In both instances, I had felt as though they were describing my story, except it was theirs.

The woman said that when she had first met Eric, he had seemed too good to be true—a politician who was interested in art and spirituality—and also, he adored her. But after a few times of making love, she said that out of nowhere, during sex, he had raised his hand up high and whacked her across the face. She said that she had tried to leave and thought she would not see him again. But the next day he had expressed remorse, and she had gone back. And then she had gotten ensnared. She said that he had tried to strangle her and she had thought, "Oh, no, this can't be how I die." She said that he had driven while intoxicated and it had been "terrifying."

In less than a year, she had broken up with him. She had had enough. A few years later, she had bumped into him at a friend's party.

He had been drunk, grabbed her arm, and said, "All right, we're going home now."

She had refused.

He had said, "Don't embarrass me in front of my security detail."

She had said, "Why don't you go home and sleep it off?"

"You know what, you were always a fucking bitch."

She told me she considered him a sociopath, narcissist, and alcoholic. She talked about the portrait of the woman in his living room, the murkily rendered portrait that had disturbed me. She wondered if it represented his mother.

She said she had wanted to reach out to me soon after the *New Yorker* article came out but had been discouraged by friends who were concerned about the potentially negative impact of publicity on her. But when she had read that I was writing a book, she figured he could come after me, and she wanted to support me.

After about an hour, I had to get back to work. We exchanged hugs and said good-bye. In the days following, I couldn't get her out of my mind. Although it had been emotionally a lot for me to hear about her experience, it had been validating in a way

I hadn't realized after all that time that I had needed. She and I both had not been prepared for the moment when our trajectory would intersect with this predator. I was hopeful that by sharing my story I could prevent such violence from happening to others.

That November, I spoke at the *Glamour* Summit on a panel with Carrie Goldberg, a victims' rights attorney, and Megan Twohey, moderated by Zain Asher of CNN. The topic was "#MeToo . . . Two Years Later." I had come a long way in terms of speaking in my own words about my story, but the summit was my first time speaking publicly before an audience about it.

The night before, I couldn't sleep. I woke up feeling shaky. I meditated, did a face mask to help with the bags under my eyes. At the event, I felt honored to be sharing the stage with those women. I asked them to sign their books for me: *She Said: Breaking the Sexual Harassment Story That Helped Ignite a Movement*, which Megan Twohey had cowritten with Jodi Kantor about breaking the Weinstein story; and *Nobody's Victim: Fighting Psychos, Stalkers, Pervs, and Trolls*, in which Carrie Goldberg detailed her own horrific experiences with intimate violence and how they had compelled her to become a lawyer who advocated for other victims. Twohey and I talked about how we had been seated next to each other at the *Glamour* Awards two years before, when I had had something I wanted to get off my chest. Things had come full circle.

I was glad I had taken the step to speak before an audience. I was buoyed by their appreciation. And I was reminded why

I was doing this work when women approached me afterward, both at the summit and via email, to tell me about how my words resonated with them and about their experiences with abuse. Many of the women were young, in their twenties—we were separated by generations, united by trauma.

The next day, at the *Glamour* Women of the Year Awards ceremony, I watched tribute videos I had made projected on the big screen at Lincoln Center. I was proud that the videos were of women speaking their truths. One honoree was the actress and producer Charlize Theron, whose mother had endured horrific domestic violence and whose new film, *Bombshell*, was about the women who had come forward and taken down Roger Ailes at Fox. The writer and artist Chanel Miller appeared to receive in person the Women of the Year honor she had been given anonymously in 2016. Everything was converging in meaningful ways.

When I wrote *The Big Lie* about my struggles with infertility, I didn't want the book to be the narrative that defined my existence. After the publicity tour was over, I returned to my work as a producer and organizer. I was happy to stop talking to the media and in front of crowds about what had been a difficult time for me, and to get back to just living and working on films and shows that had nothing to do with my personal pain. While writing this book, however, I realized that I would have to become an advocate for the long term. There is so much work to do, and I continue to find that it helps with my own healing and recovery. The previous book, and my experience with infertility, was a part of my life, but this book, this experience, will be the rest of my life.

*   *   *

In May 2020, it was time for me to finish the manuscript. I was in New York City, the epicenter of the COVID-19 pandemic in the United States. As the days went by, I started to hear about more friends who had contracted the virus and more people I knew who had died from it.

I love New York always and forever, but I wanted to be in the place where I write and heal: Portland, Oregon. My flight from JFK to PDX was canceled four times, and then I decided to take a connection through Seattle. I would be in three airports (JFK, SEA, and PDX) and taking two planes. On May 10, I took the flying challenge. I covered myself from head to toe in nonporous, waterproof material and intended not to use the bathroom on the planes. I wore welding glasses with shields at the sides of my eyes and a mask a friend had sewn for me. After I arrived, I self-quarantined for two weeks.

During my third week in Portland, a series of cataclysmic events occurred: The United States passed the devastating milestone of more than 100,000 COVID-19 deaths. Protests erupted around the country after a string of racist killings of unarmed black men and women (including George Floyd, Breonna Taylor, Sean Reed, Tony McDade, and Ahmaud Arbery), mostly by police officers. In downtown Portland, as in many other parts of the country, looters, who were not a part of the peaceful protests, escalated the violence. I received an emergency alert on my phone that a curfew had been put into place there.

About two months later, Portland became the testing ground for a new American authoritarianism, with the advent of federal law enforcement in unmarked cars and the abductions of protestors. One night, my friend Thomas was driving me home from his place, and as we passed through downtown, we came across a protest that had just been dispersed. We could detect tear gas and quickly rolled up the car windows. Officers in riot gear standing guard, protestors hunched over fleeing, storefront after storefront covered with plywood—the scene was dystopic and apocalyptic, a war zone.

I thought about James Baldwin, my father's favorite author. I had read *The Fire Next Time* to my father as he was dying. A quote by Baldwin is a continual source of inspiration for me: "The precise role of the artist, then, is to illuminate that darkness, blaze roads through that vast forest, so that we will not, in all our doing, lose sight of its purpose, which is, after all, to make the world a more human dwelling place."

In the homestretch of writing, I received an email from a woman who had been introduced by a mutual female friend to Eric Schneiderman after the *New Yorker* story came out. She and Eric had connected through their mutual interest in spirituality and healing practices. Her email contained the following statements: "I felt first drawn into the scandal as a key ally, wanting to support and believe in his innocence. I had, and have, sympathy for him. But he is a sadist and predator, and I believe, for a variety of reasons, targeted me . . . I have not been able to work with clarity since. In fact, I've been unable to breathe and think straight at times . . . I believe he has targeted me as a way to get his anger at women out."

I did not speak with her, and I can't vouch for her experience, but her note felt like an affirmation. It also sparked the first time I felt rage toward Eric. I was furious that his carefully honed world of deception had continued even after his brutal treatment of intimate partners had been exposed. I worked out my anger by focusing on turning it into light.

Another thing happened. One day on the phone with my mother, she told me, "He kicked me out of the house when I was a few months pregnant with you." She was twenty-three years old. It was near Christmas. She went to stay with a family friend. She said that soon thereafter in January "he sent me back to Sri Lanka to have you." My father didn't visit Sri Lanka for my birth. The first time he saw me was at the airport in Los Angeles when I was four months old.

I was shocked. She hadn't told me this before.

I knew it was better for my mother to be surrounded by her family in Sri Lanka rather than with my abusive father in California. But I felt unbearably sorry for her that she had to sift through memories like this about him. The pandemic had compelled us to look inward, and during this period of lockdown, my mother shared with me her truth which was indelibly intertwined with my own. I thought, "That's where the cycle of violence began for me. Even before I was born, while I was in my mother's womb, I was kicked out of the house. And now my task is to unravel this trauma."

As I wrote this epilogue, over the course of a few days, I watched a robin carry materials, pieces of fuzz and twigs, in its beak to the top of a gutter downspout on my deck. The bird was building its nest as I was finishing this book. I tried at first to watch over the nest. I wanted to protect it. I loved that little robin. But the robin seemed to be spooked by my presence, so I figured out that I had to get out of the way and let it do its thing. By the third day, the bird seemed to have gotten used to me. It didn't flee when I opened the door to the deck or when I sat down to eat at my small dining table that looked out through a window onto its nest.

I looked up information about robins, the length of their incubation and fledgling period. It seemed that we would be housemates for about a month, which was how long I had left to deliver the manuscript. It made me happy every day to look out and see the nest, a brilliant feat of engineering. I was proud of the bird that had built it. I was honored that it had chosen my house to build it on. I felt that the robin blessed my house. One night I heard little chirps coming from the nest, and I felt my heart soar. I looked up the symbolism of robins: "If the robin visits you at a certain moment of your life, then you should listen to its song. . . . [It] will help you see things from another perspective, and it will help you understand the truth." Robins signify passion, new beginnings, and renewal.

In *When Women Were Birds*, Terry Tempest Williams cited the poet Muriel Rukeyser:

"What would happen if one woman told the truth about her life?
The world would split open."

Thank you for reading my story. By doing so, you have helped me realize the power of my voice. Let's split the world open together.

APPENDIX

Jennifer Friedman, the director of the legal project at two family justice centers in New York City for Sanctuary for Families, was my sounding board and guide throughout the strenuous process of extracting myself from an abusive relationship and strategizing for my safety. We met in person in the spring of 2019 to brainstorm for this appendix. The day was May 7, exactly one year since the *New Yorker* story. (Friedman and I had picked the date by coincidence.) We began by exchanging a hug.

I asked Friedman to collaborate with me on an accessible resource for how to spot, stop, and prevent intimate partner violence. Here is her statement:

Every survivor's story is unique, and all survivors' experiences are intensely personal, often causing deep scars, physical and emotional, which can take a lifetime to heal. Despite this, there are commonalities among the stories I have heard from survivors I have encountered from all over the world. Domestic violence is one form of gender-based violence, which also includes sexual harassment, sexual assault, female genital mutilation, honor crimes, human trafficking, forced and child marriage, and others. Domestic violence involves a pattern of gender-based intimate partner, dating, or family violence with a central dynamic of power and control. In this dynamic, the abuser establishes and maintains power and asserts control over the victim/survivor. The manifestation of this dynamic can take many forms, including physical, sexual, emotional, economic, psychological, digital, and legal (discussed in this appendix).

Domestic violence is prevalent across demographic lines, including race, class, sexual orientation, and gender, although the vast majority of victims are women and girls. Not every abuser engages in physical violence. Many may use threats, such as to take the children or to hurt family members; and the weight of those threats may be effective enough so that violence is not necessary. The abuser will be extremely skilled in homing in on the victim's weaknesses and pressure points in order to exploit and manipulate her, in asserting dominance, and in enforcing compliance. This may be psychological abuse and can include exploiting a victim's history of sexual abuse to his advantage. Once women have children, this vulnerability makes them easy prey. The abusers often will use the children as pawns and leverage, even well after the relationship has ended, when there can be extensive litigation over custody, visitation, and child support. Or the abuser may construct a weakness in the victim over time, as in the case of cyber sexual abuse, where the abuser may take photographs of the victim and threaten to post them online or disseminate them to her family, community, or employer.

Many victims experience extreme trauma and may exhibit symptoms of post-traumatic stress disorder (PTSD). This is a normal psychological and physiological reaction to being threatened with death or severe harm, and is now understood to be a significant aspect of the experience of intimate partner violence. For example, the experience of being strangled, in which your air supply is cut off and you are unable to breathe, can invoke extreme trauma and PTSD.

Some victims experience a dynamic known as the "cycle of violence." There was a time when this cycle was thought to be the primary manifestation of domestic violence. While I do not see this as the only dynamic, it is a common pattern, in which there is an escalation of tension so that the victim feels she is "walking on eggshells" and that anything she does will set off the abuser. Finally, there is a violent incident that breaks the tension, and afterward there is a "honeymoon" period, in which the abuser begs for forgiveness and a break from the abuse follows. Over time, physical violence may not be as necessary because the threat is always there. The abuser has accomplished compliance.

Some domestic violence is a prelude to, or part of, sex trafficking, pimping, and commercial sexual exploitation. Many sex traffickers or pimps seek out vulnerable young people, often those who are homeless or living in group homes, and lure them into romantic relationships in which they are first courted and then subjected to intimate partner violence, groomed, and pimped.

Many survivors have their first experiences of intimate partner violence as teens or young adults. Signs of abuse in young people may be similar to those in adults but often include abuse on social media, use of photos or videos to manipulate them, excessive texting, and demanding access to passwords. College dating violence is also extremely prevalent, with nearly half of dating college women reporting the experience of abusive dating behaviors, as is sexual assault, both occurring within the context of intimate relationships and being exacerbated by partying and fraternity cultures.

There may be inherent or structural power imbalances in the relationship between victim and abuser that are easy to exploit, such as financial power, immigration status, health issues such as HIV status, and use of male, racial, or ethnic privilege. Whichever modality the abuser selects, the abuse is strategic, intended to exert control, and the victim may ultimately feel trapped in the relationship, finding it difficult, even impossible, to escape. The isolation has made her feel she has no friends or family to turn to. The sexual abuse has made her feel vulnerable and possibly ashamed. The emotional and psychological abuse has chipped away at her self-confidence, making her feel dependent or less capable than she really is. The economic abuse has possibly left her with no resources to survive on her own and take care of her children.

The threats—to kill her, to take her children, to hurt her animals or family, to expose vulnerabilities—are very effective at instilling a fear of leaving. For immigrant victims, these dynamics are exacerbated by fear of deportation, language barriers, and lack of knowledge of victims' rights within the American legal system.

Given this web of control, it is amazing that so many victims do leave and escape. Fortunately, thanks to the brave and groundbreaking work of so many leaders and feminist pioneers over the past fifty years, there are trusted resources to turn to. There are counselors and shelters, sexual assault hotlines, legal services, and some economic support resources, although certainly not enough. Included in this appendix are resources for victims in every state. I encourage anyone who reads this book and recognizes that they are in an abusive relationship to reach out to experts in the field and their community who can help develop a safety plan for their individual situation. My mantra is that because every situation is unique, it is imperative that safety planning is done individually for each victim. There isn't a cookie-cutter plan that is right for everyone. It is critical that victims and advocates be aware of danger and known lethality factors (listed in this appendix) and the reality that threats to kill can be acted upon. The most dangerous time is when the victim leaves or attempts to leave, because the abuser has lost control. This is when threats to kill become most serious and safety planning is critical.

For Tanya, there was a powerful abuser with unusual resources at his disposal. I was especially concerned about her safety. We talked at length about her knowledge of his behavior and what she believed his reactions would be to various scenarios as we planned her extraction. We asked many questions: Should she go to the police, which would trigger a criminal investigation and likely a prosecution? Should she file for a civil order of protection in family court? How could she best extricate herself? Where should she go immediately after she left, which can be the most dangerous time? Would he retaliate? If so, what form would that take? Would he physically come after her? Attack her in the street? Show up at her place of employment? Defame her to friends, family, or employers? Did he have "dirt" on her that he could try to exploit? Would he try to sabotage her employment? For victims who are financially dependent, or who have children, there are so many additional questions: Will he cut off support? Will he show up at the children's school? Try to take them away? Abduct them? File for custody? File false abuse charges against her with child protective services? Take them to another country with different laws that favor men?

The answers to these questions and many, many more will dictate the course of action that is best for each survivor. An order of protection (the name may differ by state—restraining order, protective order, etc.) can be a powerful tool, as can be filing for custody, divorce, or child support. But it is not the right move for everyone. Are you in a shelter, effectively hidden for the moment? Then perhaps filing may not be in your best interest, as the abuser would need to be served with papers and will now have the chance to locate you and retaliate. What is your economic plan for survival? Do you need child support, or should you consider filing for public assistance? Do you want or need an order of custody? Be aware that initiating a family court case could turn into a protracted battle, and the abuser will likely be granted visitation with the children. Do you know if he is planning to file for custody anyway? Then perhaps you should file first, giving yourself the opportunity to frame the narrative. Of course, it is difficult to make these decisions without legal counsel. While the costs of an attorney may be out of reach for many victims, there are organizations that provide free legal advice, which can be accessed through the resources listed here.

Your abuser may have convinced you that you have vulnerabilities he would expose in court. Talk these through with a
lawyer, if possible. It may be that there are real legal challenges,
or it may be that he has manipulated you into believing that he
has advantages that are not in fact legally compelling. You may
also have rights you were unaware of. If you are an immigrant
survivor, there are pathways to legal residency separate from
the abuser, such as asylum, a Violence Against Women Act
Self-Petition (aka battered spouse waiver), a U visa, a T visa, or
Special Immigrant Juvenile Status (SIJS).

In any case, my strongest advice is to reach out, if possible,
to one of the resources provided here and, when you feel ready,
safely speak with someone who can help provide you with options you may not have known existed. You are the expert in
your own situation. Your intuition is there for a reason, and you
should use it to help guide you through this entire process. If
you are receiving advice you doubt, perhaps you should get a
second opinion. You know the pressure points and the danger
you are in, and you should not allow anyone to convince you
to do anything that you are not ready for. Ultimately, no one
except you walks in your shoes.

All survivors have to decide for themselves whether and
when they are ready to share their stories and possibly seek
help. No matter how humiliating you may think your situation is, coming forward and speaking your truth, if only to
a counselor or lawyer, is extraordinarily brave and can bring
about a breakthrough. The abuser has sought to silence your
voice and diminish your self-worth, preventing you from feeling your own power. But you *do* have power, and seeking help

(including speaking with an expert) may bring you more power. Taking back your power is an important step toward healing and reclaiming your life. While the larger society may not honor women's voices because of an entrenched power structure dominated primarily by men, times are changing.

—Jennifer Friedman, Director, Bronx and Manhattan Legal Project and Policy, Sanctuary for Families

I. SIGNS OF INTIMATE PARTNER VIOLENCE

The following is adapted from B. J. Cling and Dorchen A. Leidholdt, "Interviewing and Assisting Domestic Violence Survivors," in *Lawyer's Manual on Domestic Violence: Representing the Victim*, 6th ed., edited by Mary Rothwell Davis, Dorchen A. Leidholdt, and Charlotte A. Watson (Supreme Court of the State of New York, 2015), http://ww2.nycourts.gov/sites/default /files/document/files/2018-07/DV-Lawyers-Manual-Book.pdf.

Jealousy and Possessiveness

Jealousy and possessiveness are two of the most common characteristics of abusers. These may initially be interpreted by the victim as signs of her partner's passion and devotion, though it soon becomes apparent that they underlie his acts of domination and control. The jealousy can take many different forms. An abuser may use GPS to monitor a victim, accuse her of having affairs with every man in her life, call the victim frequently during the day, send constant text messages, drop by her place of work unexpectedly, prevent her from performing her job effectively, check her car's mileage, or ask friends or neighbors to watch her.

Controlling Behavior

This is a hallmark of abuse, which may be related to jealousy and can permeate every facet of existence. An abuser will initially attribute his controlling behavior to concern for her well-being. The situation will progressively worsen. The abuser may ultimately monitor her every move, assume control of all finances, and/or prevent the victim from coming and going freely.

Quick Involvement

A victim often knows or dates the abuser for a brief, intense period of time before getting engaged or moving in together. Almost immediately in their relationship, the abuser will pressure the victim to commit to him and will make her feel guilty for wanting to slow the pace. The abuser expects the partner to meet all his needs, build her world around him, and submerge her identity in his.

Manipulative Behavior

Abusers are often skilled manipulators who begin by appearing to be devoted, dependable partners. Once a victim is entrapped in the relationship and tries to get out, the abuser may manipulate the very agencies the victim can turn to for help, such as criminal justice, child welfare, and judicial authorities. Often the abuser will succeed in having his victim investigated for child abuse or neglect, arrested for fabricated crimes, or tarred as an alienating parent. An abuser will also manipulate his children, persuading them that their mother is to blame for the family's no longer living together or for their moving from their old neighborhood or school.

Isolation

Abusers isolate their victims by severing the victims' ties to outside support and resources. The abuser will create conflict with the victim's friends and family, forcing the victim to choose between them and him. The abuser may block the victim's access to use of a vehicle, work, or telephone and internet service in the home. He wants her in the home, where she is totally under his control, so any social contact becomes a threat.

Blame and Incessant Criticism

The abuser is never at fault and never accepts responsibility for his actions, blaming others for his own shortcomings. He will blame the victim for almost anything, including his poor work performance, his bad relationships with other people, and, above all, his violence toward her.

Abusive and Violent Sex

Sexual abuse is a pervasive form of domestic violence. This includes forcing unwanted sex, restraining partners against their will during sex, acting out fantasies in which the partner is helpless, initiating sex when the partner is asleep, or demanding sex when the partner is ill or tired.

Verbal Abuse

Abusers usually subject their victims to an unending barrage of insults. The epithets "bitch" and "whore" are staples among abusers, as are threats and obscenities. The language the abuser uses can be cruel and hurtful, including cursing, degrading, or insulting the victim or putting down the victim's accomplishments.

Rigid Gender Roles

Abusers often demand that their partners conform to traditional sex or gender roles. The victim is supposed to be passive, obedient, solicitous, attractive, a great cook who always has dinner on the table just when he is ready for it, and sexually available to him whenever he is in the mood. Many abusers move to control the family's finances and discourage or undermine their victims' educational and career aspirations; they maintain that marriage gives them full authority over the victim and the family.

Dual Personality: "Dr. Jekyll and Mr. Hyde"

Abusers often exhibit different personalities at different times, leaving the victims to tiptoe around them and guess which person they will get at any given moment. At times, the abuser can be loving and at other times cruel. Explosive behavior and moodiness can shift quickly into congeniality.

Past Battering

A victim will often discover that the abuser's past relationships followed a pattern of abuse similar to hers. (Individual occurrences do not constitute an abusive personality.)

Threats of Violence

These consist of any threat of physical force meant to control the partner.

Breaking or Striking Objects

This behavior is used as punishment (e.g., breaking sentimental possessions) or to terrorize the victim into submission.

Cruelty to Animals

An abuser will injure or even kill beloved family pets as a sign of his power, as a threat of violence toward the family, or simply as an act of cruelty.

Use of Privilege

The abuser will use whatever leverage he has against the victim, including social status, financial status, male privilege, race privilege, immigration status, and knowledge of the victim's personal information, such as gender identity, sexual orientation, or religious status. This may take the form of emotional or psychological abuse, with name-calling, demeaning, or degrading the victim based on status or lack of privilege. Male privilege may include using rigid sex roles as a means of control, such as demanding sex as a marital right. In LGBTQIA+ relationships, there may be threats to out the victim to friends, family, or colleagues. Where the victim is undocumented or not a US citizen, there may be threats to report the victim to US Immigration and Customs Enforcement (ICE) or other authorities.

II. TYPES OF ABUSE AND THEIR EFFECTS

The following is adapted from Dorchen Leidholdt, Esq., and Ted McCourtney, MSW, "Understanding Domestic Violence," an unpublished PowerPoint presentation.

Types of Abuse

Physical Abuse

- Hitting, slapping, shoving, grabbing, pinching, biting, and pulling hair
- Choking you or trying to suffocate you
- Preventing access to medical care
- Having easy access to weapons
- Forcing you to use alcohol or drugs
- Driving dangerously while you are in the car

Sexual Abuse

- Holding you down during sex
- Forcing you to have sex or making you do other sexual acts unwillingly
- Forcing you to have sex after hurting you or when you are sick or tired
- Calling you sexual names or forcing you to dress in a certain way
- Assaulting your genital area or breasts
- Pressuring/demanding that you have sex with other people
- Forcing you to watch or act out pornography
- Taking sexual/pornographic photographs of you and using them to manipulate your behavior, such as threatening to release them to friends and family or post them online

Emotional Abuse

- Name-calling or insulting you
- Acting jealous and not trusting you

- Humiliating you
- Making you question your perception of reality within a relationship by using statements such as "That never happened" or "It's all in your head" (aka gaslighting)
- Cheating on you repeatedly and then blaming you for the infidelity
- Damaging your relationships with your children

Economic Abuse

- Withholding access to your money
- Refusing to let you go to work or school
- Forcing you to mount up debt to hurt your credit
- Refusing you access to money for necessities such as food and medical care
- Preventing you from viewing bank accounts
- Signing your name on financial instruments, such as rent, mortgages, car loans, and other documents, without your knowledge or against your will
- Allowing you to work but confiscating your paycheck
- Giving you a limited budget and forcing you to account for every penny spent

Psychological Abuse

- Intimidating you
- Isolating you from other people
- Threatening to harm people you care about or pets
- Threatening to take your children
- Stalking you: following; sending unsolicited letters,

messages, and/or gifts; destroying or vandalizing your property; threatening to harm your family members or friends

- Controlling your reproductive freedom by forcing sex, denying you access to contraceptives or abortion

Digital Abuse

- Controlling your passwords
- Searching your phone often, including texts and calls
- Monitoring you with any technology, such as a GPS
- Insulting you in social media status updates
- Engaging in cyber sexual abuse (also known as "revenge porn")
- Spoofing (setting up a false online profile of you intended to destroy your reputation)
- Installing spyware on your devices to intercept communication and personal information
- Sending defamatory messages about you through email and/or social networking websites

Legal Abuse

- Falsely reporting you to law enforcement or child welfare agencies
- Threatening deportation
- Initiating retaliatory cases, such as filing orders of protection, suing for custody, and making frivolous claims
- After the relationship has ended, gaining access to you by engaging in litigation
- Instituting legal proceedings that you cannot afford to fight

Effects of Abuse

Physical Effects

- Direct physical injury: bruises, broken bones, lacerations, traumatic brain injury, vision and hearing impairment, damage to or loss of teeth
- Other physical effects: chronic headaches, pervasive body aches, feelings of dizziness
- Insomnia and disrupted or abnormal sleep
- Long-term physical effects: chronic illnesses such as heart disease (in middle-aged and old survivors), diabetes, autoimmune disorders, and stroke

Psychological Effects

- High levels of anxiety
- Depression
- Minimization/denial
- Numbness/flattened affect
- Memory loss
- Dissociation
- Shame, self-blame
- Self-medication (drug/alcohol abuse)
- Post-traumatic stress disorder (PTSD)
- Intrusion: emotional reactions, flashbacks, images, nightmares
- Avoidance: dissociation, minimizing, numbing, denial
- Arousal: anger, difficulty concentrating or sleeping

Lethality Indicators

- Increase in severity or frequency of violence
- Use of or threats to use weapons
- Threats to kill you, children, and/or self
- Abuse of drugs or alcohol
- Stalking, choking, or forced sex
- Unemployment
- Separation

III. RESOURCES

Whether you are a victim or a loved one seeking to support a victim, there are organizations you can turn to for help and information. What follows is a range of national and community-specific options. Several of the national organizations listed here include state-specific resources.

Resources for Immediate Safety Assistance

National Domestic Violence Hotline

> https://www.thehotline.org
> National Domestic Violence Hotline, P.O. Box 90249,
> Austin, TX 78709
> Hotline: 1-800-799-7233
> TTY: 1-800-787-3224
> Office: 1-512-453-8117

"Operating around the clock, seven days a week, confidential and free of cost, the National Domestic Violence Hotline provides lifesaving tools and immediate support to enable victims to find safety and live lives free of abuse."

Family Justice Center Alliance

https://www.familyjusticecenter.org
Alliance for HOPE International, 101 W. Broadway,
    Suite 1770, San Diego, CA 92101
Office: 1-888-511-3522
List of affiliated centers: https://www.familyjusticecenter.org
/affiliated-centers

"The Family Justice Center Alliance (FJCA) is a program of Alliance for HOPE International, one of the leading domestic violence and sexual assault prevention and intervention organizations in the United States. The FJCA serves as the clearinghouse, research center, and national affiliation organization for Family Justice Centers and other multi-agency centers that serve victims of domestic violence, sexual assault, elder abuse, child abuse, and/or human trafficking."

Family Justice Centers provide assistance with shelter, counseling, legal, and other services. Most are designed as walk-in centers that can be accessed by any victim in need. The link given here provides information about centers located throughout the United States.

RAINN (Rape, Abuse & Incest National Network)

> https://www.rainn.org
> Hotline: 1-800-656-4673
> Office: 1-202-544-1034

"RAINN (Rape, Abuse & Incest National Network) is the nation's largest anti-sexual violence organization. RAINN created and operates the National Sexual Assault Hotline (800.656.HOPE, online.rainn.org or rainn.org/es) in partnership with more than 1,000 local sexual assault service providers across the country and operates the DoD Safe Helpline for the Department of Defense. RAINN also carries out programs to prevent sexual violence, help survivors, and ensure that perpetrators are brought to justice."

Legal Resources

*American Bar Association Commission
on Domestic & Sexual Violence*

> https://www.americanbar.org/groups/domestic_violence

"Our mission is to increase access to justice for victims of domestic violence, sexual assault and stalking by mobilizing the legal profession." The ABA Commission on Domestic & Sexual Violence provides individualized support to attorneys representing victims of domestic violence, sexual assault, and stalking, including research assistance, sample practice tools, model pleadings, and access to experts in the field.

ImmigrationLawHelp.org

https://www.immigrationlawhelp.org

"ImmigrationLawHelp.org is a searchable online directory of over 1,000 free or low-cost nonprofit immigration legal services providers in all 50 states. Only nonprofits that are BIA recognized or have attorneys on staff are included in the directory. Users can search ImmigrationLawHelp.org by state, zip code, or detention facility. Users can also refine their search by types and areas of legal assistance provided, populations served, languages spoken, other areas of legal assistance, and non-legal services provided. ImmigrationLawHelp .org was developed by the Immigration Advocates Network and Pro Bono Net with support from the Four Freedoms Fund."

National Institute of Justice Violence Against Women and Family Violence Program

https://www.nij.gov/topics/crime/violence-against-women /pages/welcome.aspx

"The mission of the Violence Against Women and Family Violence Research and Evaluation program is to promote the safety of women and family members, and to increase the efficiency and effectiveness of the criminal justice system's response to these crimes. This mission is being accomplished through the following objectives:

- **Estimating the Scope of the Problem** to understand the extent of violence against women and family members . . .

- **Identifying Causes and Consequences** to identify the reasons violent behavior against women and within the family occur . . .
- **Evaluating Promising Prevention and Intervention Programs.**"

National Women's Law Center

> https://nwlc.org
> National Women's Law Center, 11 DuPont Circle NW,
>   Suite 800, Washington, DC 20036
> Office: 1-202-588-5180

"The National Women's Law Center fights for gender justice—in the courts, in public policy, and in our society—working across the issues that are central to the lives of women and girls. We use the law in all its forms to change culture and drive solutions to the gender inequity that shapes our society and to break down the barriers that harm all of us—especially those who face multiple forms of discrimination, including women of color, LGBTQ people, and low-income women and families. For more than 45 years, we have been on the leading edge of every major legal and policy victory for women."

WomensLaw.org

> https://www.womenslaw.org

"Despite its name, WomensLaw.org provides information that is relevant to people of all genders, not just women. Our Email Hotline will provide legal information to anyone who reaches out with legal questions or concerns regarding domestic violence, sexual violence, or any other topic covered on WomensLaw.org." [Also see the Family Justice Center Alliance.]

Community-Specific Resources

Asian/Pacific Islander Domestic Violence Resource Project

https://dvrp.org
A/PI DVRP, P.O. Box 14268, Washington, DC 20044
Hotline: 1-202-833-2233
Office: 1-202-833-2232
Email: info@dvrp.org

"The Asian/Pacific Islander Domestic Violence Resource Project (DVRP) is a non-profit organization in Washington, DC. Our mission is to address, prevent, and end domestic violence and sexual assault in Asian/Pacific Islander communities while empowering survivors to rebuild their lives after abuse."

Black Women's Blueprint

https://www.blackwomensblueprint.org
Black Women's Blueprint, 279 Empire Blvd.,
    Brooklyn, NY 11225
Office: 1-347-533-9102/3
Email: info@blueprintny.org

Black Women's Blueprint specializes in providing "help for women, cis, trans and LGBTQ survivors of sexual assault, rape, childhood sexual and/or physical abuse, human trafficking, and physical assault."

Break the Cycle

http://www.breakthecycle.org
Break the Cycle, P.O. Box 66165, Washington, DC 20035
Text: loveis to 22522
Office: 1-202-849-6289

"Break the Cycle inspires and supports young people 12–24 to build healthy relationships and create a culture without abuse. We are a culturally affirming organization that centers young people, caring adults, and communities in our prevention and intervention efforts."

Casa de Esperanza

https://casadeesperanza.org
Casa de Esperanza, P.O. Box 40115, St. Paul, MN 55104
Minnesota crisis line: 1-651-772-1611
National hotline: 1-800-799-7233
Office: 1-651-646-5553
Email: info@casadeesperanza.org

"Casa de Esperanza is a leader in the domestic violence movement and a national resource center for organizations working with Latin@s in the United States. Based in St. Paul, Minnesota Casa de Esperanza's mission is to 'mobilize Latinas and Latin@ communities to end domestic violence.' Founded in 1982 to provide emergency shelter for Latinas and other women and children experiencing domestic violence, the organization has grown to become the largest Latina organization in the country focused on domestic violence. Casa de Esperanza is also committed to becoming a greater resource to organizations and communities in the areas of sexual assault and trafficking."

Day One

https://www.dayoneny.org
Day One, P.O. Box 3220, Church Street Station,
    New York, NY 10008
Hotline: 1-800-214-4150
Text: 1-646-535-3291
Email: info@dayoneny.org

"Our mission is to partner with youth to end dating abuse and domestic violence through community education, supportive services, legal advocacy and leadership development."

Daya

https://www.dayahouston.org
Daya, Inc., P.O. Box 770773, Houston, TX 77215
Hotline: 1-713-981-7645
Office: 1-713-842-7222
Email: contact@dayahouston.org

"Daya's mission is to empower South Asian survivors of domestic and sexual violence through culturally specific services and to educate the community in an effort to end the cycle of abuse."

National Coalition of Anti-Violence Programs

> https://avp.org/ncavp
> National Coalition of Anti-Violence Programs,
>   116 Nassau Street, 3rd floor, New York, NY 10038
> Bilingual hotline: 1-212-714-1141
> Office: 1-212-714-1184

"We work to prevent, respond to, and end all forms of violence against and within LGBTQ communities. We're a national coalition of local member programs, affiliate organizations and individual affiliates who create systemic and social change. We strive to increase power, safety and resources through data analysis, policy advocacy, education and technical assistance."

National Deaf Domestic Violence Hotline

> https://thedeafhotline.org
> Hotline: 1-800-799-7233
> TTY: 1-800-787-3224
> Videophone: 1-855-812-1001
> Email: nationaldeafhotline@adwas.org

"All survivors of domestic violence face the same issue: abuse thrives in isolation. This can be especially true for survivors of domestic violence who are Deaf, DeafBlind or hard of hearing. Domestic violence programs can still isolate survivors by not providing adequate access to critical information.

"Our hotline strives to educate the public about the need for Deaf, DeafBlind and hard of hearing abuse outreach programs.

The safe and strictly confidential services that our hotline offers Deaf survivors can be life-saving."

National Indigenous Women's Resource Center

http://www.niwrc.org
National Indigenous Women's Resource Center, 515 Lame
    Deer Avenue, P.O. Box 99, Lame Deer, MT 59043
Office: 1-406-477-3896
Toll-Free: 1-855-649-7299

"The National Indigenous Women's Resource Center, Inc. (NIWRC) is a Native nonprofit organization that was created specifically to serve as the National Indian Resource Center (NIRC) Addressing Domestic Violence and Safety for Indian Women."

National LGBTQ Institute on IPV

https://lgbtqipv.org

"The LBGTQ Institute on IPV expands the capacity of individuals, organizations, governmental agencies, local communities, tribes, and tribal organizations to identify and respond to the specific and emerging needs of diverse LGBTQ intimate partner violence survivors. We inform research and policy agendas, coordinate with other Domestic Violence Resource Network members, and provide training and technical assistance to improve violence prevention and intervention efforts nationwide."

Operation Restoration

https://or-nola.org
Operation Restoration, 1450 Poydras St., Suite 2260,
    New Orleans, LA 70112
Office: 1-504-684-9222
Email: info@or-nola.org

"Operation Restoration supports women and girls impacted by incarceration to recognize their full potential, restore their lives, and discover new possibilities. . . . One of OR's greatest strengths is that it is an organization created by and for formerly incarcerated women."

Peaceful Families Project

https://www.peacefulfamilies.org
Peaceful Families Project, P.O. Box 771, Great Falls, VA 22066
Office: 1-540-324-8818
Email: info@peacefulfamilies.org

"Our mission is to work towards preventing all types of abuse in Muslim families by increasing awareness regarding the dynamics of domestic violence. We believe that a better understanding of religious and cultural values can be used as a resource to prevent domestic violence, and that religion and culture should never be used to justify abusive behavior. Through education and training, we seek to promote attitudes and beliefs that emphasize justice, freedom from oppression, and family harmony."

Sanctuary for Families

https://sanctuaryforfamilies.org
Sanctuary for Families, P.O. Box 1406, Wall Street Station,
New York, NY 10268
Legal hotline: 1-212-249-6009, ext. 246
Text: 1-646-692-0300
Email: info@sffny.org

"Sanctuary for Families is dedicated to the safety, healing and self-determination of victims of domestic violence and related forms of gender violence. Through comprehensive services for our clients and their children, and through outreach, education and advocacy, we strive to create a world in which freedom from gender violence is a basic human right."

StrongHearts Native Helpline

https://www.strongheartshelpline.org
Hotline: 1-844-7NATIVE (762-8483)
Email: info@strongheartshelpline.org

"StrongHearts Native Helpline is a safe domestic violence and dating violence helpline for American Indians and Alaska Natives, offering culturally-appropriate support and advocacy daily from 7 a.m. to 10 p.m. CT. Anonymous and confidential.

Callers reaching out after hours may connect with the National Domestic Violence Hotline by selecting option one. StrongHearts is a project of the National Domestic Violence Hotline and the National Indigenous Women's Resource Center."

Trans Lifeline

> https://translifeline.org
> Trans Lifeline, 195 41st St., #11253, Oakland,
>   CA 94611-9991
> Hotline: 1-877-565-8860
> Office: 1-510-771-1417
> Email: contact@translifeline.org

"Trans Lifeline is a grassroots hotline and microgrants 503(c) (3) non-profit organization offering direct emotional and financial support to trans people in crisis—for the trans community, by the trans community.

"Trans Lifeline was founded in 2014 as a peer-support crisis hotline. The Hotline was, and still is, the only service in the country in which all operators are transgender. Because of the particularly vulnerable relationship transgender people have with police, it is also the only service in the country with a policy against non-consensual active rescue."

Ujima: The National Center on Violence Against Women in the Black Community

> https://ujimacommunity.org
> Hotline: 1-800-799-7233
> Office: 1-844-77-UJIMA (85462)
> Email: ujimainfo@ujimacommunity.org

"The mission of the National Center on Violence Against Women in the Black Community is to mobilize the community to respond to and end domestic, sexual and community violence in the Black community."

Additional Resources

A Call to Men

https://www.acalltomen.org
Office: 1-917-922-6738
Email: info@acalltomen.org

"A CALL TO MEN is a violence prevention organization and respected leader on issues of manhood, male socialization and its intersection with violence, and preventing violence against all women and girls."

Equality Now

https://www.equalitynow.org
Equality Now, 125 Maiden Lane, 9th Floor, Suite B,
   New York, NY 10038
Office: 1-212-586-0906

"At Equality Now, we believe in creating a just world where women and girls have the same rights as men and boys. We tackle the most difficult issues, challenge ingrained cultural assumptions and call out inequality wherever we see it. . . . we use the power of the law to create enduring equality for women and girls everywhere."

FreeFrom

> http://www.freefrom.org
> FreeFrom, 12405 Venice Blvd., Suite 422,
>   Los Angeles, CA 90066

"Our mission is to create pathways to financial security and long-term safety that support survivors of gender-based violence."

Futures Without Violence

> https://www.futureswithoutviolence.org
> Futures Without Violence, 100 Montgomery St.,
>   The Presidio, San Francisco, CA 94129
> Office: 1-415-678-5500
> Email: info@futureswithoutviolence.org

"For more than 30 years, FUTURES has been providing groundbreaking programs, policies, and campaigns that empower individuals and organizations working to end violence against women and children around the world.

"Providing leadership from offices in San Francisco, Washington D.C. and Boston, we've established a state-of-the-art Center for Leadership and Action in the Presidio of San Francisco to foster ongoing dialogue about gender-based violence and child abuse."

A Long Walk Home

http://www.alongwalkhome.org
A Long Walk Home, 1658 N. Milwaukee Ave.,
   Suite 104, Chicago, IL 60647
Office: 1-877-571-1751
Email: info@alongwalkhome.org

"A Long Walk Home empowers young artists and activists to end violence against all girls and women. We advocate for racial and gender equity in schools, communities, and our country-at-large."

National Coalition Against Domestic Violence

http://www.ncadv.org
NCADV, 600 Grant, Suite 750, Denver, CO 80203
Office: 1-303-839-1852

"The National Coalition Against Domestic Violence (NCADV)'s mission is to lead, mobilize and raise our voices to support efforts that demand a change of conditions that lead to domestic violence such as patriarchy, privilege, racism, sexism, and classism. We are dedicated to supporting survivors and holding offenders accountable and supporting advocates."

National Disability Rights Network

https://www.ndrn.org
National Disability Rights Network, 820 First St. NE,
   Suite 740, Washington, DC 20002
Office: 1-202-408-9514

"The National Disability Rights Network works in Washington, DC on behalf of the Protection and Advocacy Systems (P&As) and Client Assistance Programs (CAPs), the nation's largest providers of legal advocacy services for people with disabilities."

National Network to End Domestic Violence

https://nnedv.org
National Network to End Domestic Violence,
    1325 Massachusetts Ave. NW, 7th Floor,
    Washington, DC 20005
Hotline: 1-800-7999-7233
Office: 1-202-543-5566
Technology Safety: https://www.techsafety.org

"The National Network to End Domestic Violence (NNEDV) is a social change organization dedicated to creating a social, political, and economic environment in which violence against women no longer exists."

The Polaris Project

https://polarisproject.org
Polaris, P.O. Box 65323, Washington, DC 20035
Hotline: 1-888-373-7888
Office: 1-202-790-6300
Email: info@polarisproject.org

"Founded in 2002, Polaris is named for the North Star, which people held in slavery in the United States used as a guide to navigate their way toward freedom. Today we are filling in the roadmap for that journey and lighting the path ahead." The

Polaris Project serves victims and survivors through the National Human Trafficking Hotline; builds a dataset that illuminates how trafficking really works, in real time; and turns knowledge into targeted systems-level strategies to disrupt and prevent human trafficking.

UN Women

https://www.unwomen.org/en
UN Women, 220 East 42nd St., New York, NY 10017
Office: 1-646-781-4400

"UN Women is the United Nations entity dedicated to gender equality and the empowerment of women. . . .

"UN Women supports UN Member States as they set global standards for achieving gender equality, and works with governments and civil society to design laws, policies, programmes and services needed to ensure that the standards are effectively implemented and truly benefit women and girls worldwide."

ACKNOWLEDGMENTS

Infinite thanks to:

My literary agent, Meg Thompson; editor, Lisa Sharkey; publisher, Jonathan Burnham; and everyone at Harper, especially Tina Andreadis, Leslie Cohen, and Maddie Pillari for their incredible support.

Cindi Leive for helping me have the courage to tell my story.

David Remnick, Jane Mayer, Ronan Farrow, Jyoti Thottam, Marin Cogan, and Amelia Schonbek for the care they gave my story.

Julie Fink, Jennifer Friedman, Roberta Kaplan, Tim Miller, Rachel Tuchman, Rita Glavin, Sharon Nelles, Dorchen Leidholdt, and Wilder Knight for their counsel and guidance when I came forward and in the aftermath.

Libby Burton for her editing of an early iteration of the manuscript and her continued allyship throughout the book's journey.

Joanna Coles for championing this book and helping it find a home.

Arthur Bradford, Julia Chaplin, Farai Chideya, Jenny Davidson, Kiran Desai, Eamon Dolan, Mark Epstein, Tyler Gray, Jennifer Gonnerman, Catherine Gund, Dan Harris, Yasmeen Hassan, Rujeko Hockley, A. M. Homes, Larissa MacFarquhar, Sia Michel, Kiele Raymond, Danzy Senna, Tiffany Shlain, Andrew Solomon, Elliot Thomson, and Carrie Mae Weems for their feedback on my writing.

Béatrice de Géa, K. K. Ottesen, and Damon Winter for their photographs.

Ciara Alfaro, Clare Frucht, and Jillian Mannarino for their research assistance.

All my family, friends, and colleagues for their comfort and insights, including Laurie Anderson, Frank Andrews, Chloe Aridjis, Eva Aridjis, Zain Asher, De'Ara Balenger, Lyndon Barrois, Jr., Samantha Barry, Elizabeth Bawol, Mikaela Beardsley, Gina Belafonte, Ginia Bellafante, Megan Beyer, Jennie Boddy, Jennifer Braunschweiger, Nell Breyer, Isolde Brielmaier, Winsome Brown, Heather Carlucci, Melissa Ceria, Elaine Chen, Gabri Christa, Marsha Cooke, Lisa Cortés, Sue Craig, Amy Davidson, Celine DeCarlo, Joy de Menil, Sonali Deraniyagala, Nicolette Donen, Sarah Dougher, Geralyn White Dreyfous, Sandi DuBowski, Sarah Ellison, Wendy Ettinger, Ellen Fanning, John Fleck, Sarah Sophie Flicker, Miriam Fogelson, China Forbes, Shari Frilot, C. J. Frogozo, Shruti Ganguly, Caryn Ganz, Liz Garbus, Carrie Goldberg, Leah Greenblatt, Vanessa Grigoriadis, Agnes Gund, Justine Harman, Virginia Heffernan, Priyanka Chopra Jonas, Hillary Jordan, Mattie Kahn, Sibyl Kempson, Rachna Khare, Kim Krans, Sarah Lash, Thomas Lauderdale, Sarah Lewis, Lauren Lumsden, Alex and Vida Marashian, Eve Samborn McCool, Dyllan McGee, Elizabeth

Cronise McLaughlin, Suketu Mehta, Elizabeth Méndez Berry, Paola Mendoza, Liz Mermin, Laura Michalchyshyn, Debbie Millman, Unjoo Moon, Walter Mosley, Wendy Naugle, Marie Nelson, Emily Oberman, Molly O'Brien, Andrew Ondrejcak, Sherwin Parikh, Natasha Pearlman, Lindsay Pera, Evgenia Peretz, Chrysi Philalithes, Lydia Pilcher, Gabriela Poma, Alissa Quart, Linda Rattner, Amy Richards, Mary Rohlich, Hannah Rosenzweig, Melena Ryzik, Wendy Sachs, Miguel Sancho, Gina Sanders, Therese Selvaratnam, Troy Selvaratnam, Wendy Shanker, Fiona Shaw, Meredith Shepherd, Heidi Sieck, Melissa Silverstein, Mark Skidmore, Mary Skinner, Amy Lou Stein, Ginny Suss, Hank Willis Thomas, Ellyn Toscano, Megan Twohey, Kate Valk, Lucy Walker, Kristina Wallison, Tamara Warren, Jessica Whitaker, Deborah Willis, Sara Wolitzky, Soon-Young Yoon, and Julie Zann.

The women who came forward with me; the women and men who have come forward with their stories; and the journalists and writers who have shown that, taking a cue from Naomi Alderman, we can understand our strength all at once.

NOTES

INTRODUCTION

xvii   In one year, this equates to: "National Statistics," National Coalition Against Domestic Violence, https://ncadv.org/statistics.

CHAPTER 1: THE FAIRY TALE

4   "the man the banks fear most": Harold Meyerson, "The Man the Banks Fear Most," *The American Prospect*, April 23, 2012, https://prospect.org/power/man-banks-fear/.

4   "transforming the liberal checklist": Eric Schneiderman, "Transforming the Liberal Checklist," *The Nation*, February 21, 2008, https://www.thenation.com/article/transforming-liberal-checklist.

CHAPTER 2: ENTRAP

16   "Those with NPD": Beverly Engel, *The Emotionally Abusive Relationship: How to Stop Being Abused and How to Stop Abusing* (Hoboken, NJ: John Wiley and Sons, 2002), 204.

16   "Too much closeness terrifies": Ibid., 205.

CHAPTER 4: CONTROL

41   "the Dear Reader": Margaret Atwood, *The Handmaid's Tale* (New York: Anchor Books, 1986), xviii.

CHAPTER 5: DEMEAN

46   "If you find yourself": Eileen Hoenigman Meyer, "How to Deal When a Colleague Is Threatened by You," Glassdoor, May 11, 2018, https://www.glassdoor.com/blog/threatened.

47   "To make contemporary women": Evan Stark, *Coercive Control: How Men Entrap Women in Personal Life* (New York: Oxford University Press, 2007), 197.

47   "Verbal abuse is secretive": Patricia Evans, *The Verbally Abusive Relationship: How to Recognize It and How to Respond* (New York: Adams Media, 2010), 21.

48   "Verbal abuse is, in a sense": Ibid.

51   "Without an 'audience'": Stark, *Coercive Control*, 110.

CHAPTER 6: ABUSE

55   "What's going on": Margaret Atwood, *The Handmaid's Tale* (New York: Anchor Books, 1986), 94.

57   "essentially a junk drawer": David J. Morris, *The Evil Hours: A Biography of Post-Traumatic Stress Disorder* (New York: Eamon Dolan Books, 2015), 13–14.

58   "that there is no": Patricia Evans, *The Verbally Abusive Relationship: How to Recognize It and How to Respond* (New York: Adams Media, 2010), 101–02.

60   "You're picturing": Megan McArdle, "I Went Back to a Man Who Hit Me. I'm Still Thinking About Why," *Washington Post*, May 8, 2018, https://www.washingtonpost.com/opinions/i-went-back-to-the-man-who-hit-me-why/2018/05/08/0acb4c54-52f2-11e8-abd8-265bd07a9859_story.html.

CHAPTER 7: THE NIGHTMARE

62   "when it comes to danger": Gavin de Becker, *The Gift of Fear: And Other Survival Signals That Protect Us from Violence* (New York: Dell Publishing, 1997), 71.

65   Burkle's private plane: Vanessa Grigoriadis, "'I Collect People, I Own People, I Can Damage People': The Curious Sociopathy of Jeffrey Epstein," *Vanity Fair*, August 26, 2019, https://www.vanityfair.com/news/2019/08/curious-sociopathy-of-jeffrey-epstein-ex-girlfriends.

65   Megan Twohey wrote: Megan Twohey, "Tumult After AIDS Fund-Raiser Supports Harvey Weinstein Production," *New York Times*, September 23, 2017, https://www.nytimes.com/2017/09/23/nyregion/harvey-weinstein-charity.html.

66   "*Vanity Fair*'s subsequent piece": William D. Cohan, "'Nothing About This Deal Feels Right to Me': Inside Harvey Weinstein's Other Nightmare," *Vanity Fair*, December 20, 2017, https://www.vanityfair.com/news/2017/12/harvey-weinstein-nightmare-finding-neverland-amfar-money.

66   Thereafter, internet searches: Amy B. Wang, "'Complicit' Is the 2017 Word of the Year, According to Dictionary.com," *Washington Post*, November 27,

2017, https://www.washingtonpost.com/news/the-intersect/wp/2017/11/27
/complicit-is-the-2017-word-of-the-year-according-to-dictionary-com.

68   "[Physical abuse] is most often": Rachel Louise Snyder, *No Visible Bruises:
What We Don't Know About Domestic Violence Can Kill Us* (New York: Bloomsbury Publishing, 2019), 10.

68   "This first stage of recognition": Patricia Evans, *The Verbally Abusive Relationship: How to Recognize It and How to Respond* (New York: Adams Media,
2010), 113.

69   "More than one in every four": Emma M. Millon, Han Yan M. Chang,
and Tracey J. Shors, "Stressful Life Memories Relate to Ruminative Thoughts
in Women with Sexual Violence History, Irrespective of PTSD," *Frontiers in
Psychiatry*, September 5, 2018, https://www.frontiersin.org/articles/10.3389
/fpsyt.2018.00311/full.

70   "Victims of sexual violence": Jessica Ravitz and Arman Azad, "Memories That Last: What Sexual Assault Survivors Remember and Why," CNN,
September 21, 2018, https://www.cnn.com/2018/09/21/health/memory-sexual
-assault-ptsd/index.html.

CHAPTER 8: WHAT IS INTIMATE VIOLENCE?

71   "Intimate violence" is a subset: According to the World Health Organization, "Research suggests that physical violence in intimate relationships is
often accompanied by psychological abuse, and in one-third to over one-half
of cases by sexual abuse." World Health Organization, "Violence by Intimate
Partners," in *World Report on Violence and Health*, ed. Etienne G. Krug, Linda L.
Dahlberg, James A. Mercy, Anthony B. Zwi, and Rafael Lozano (Geneva:
World Health Organization, 2002), http://www.who.int/violence_injury
_prevention/violence/global_campaign/en/chap4.pdf, 89.

72   "About 1 in 4 women": "Preventing Intimate Partner Violence," Atlanta:
Centers for Disease Control and Prevention, 2019, https://www.cdc.gov/violence
prevention/pdf/ipv-factsheet508.pdf, 1.

72   the vast majority of violence: According to FBI records of ten-year
arrest trends between 2008 and 2017, 87 percent of murders and non-
negligent manslaughters, 97 percent of rapes, and 76.8 percent of aggravated
assaults were committed by men. Globally, almost 30 percent of women
have experienced intimate partner violence, and as many as 38 percent of
murders of women are committed by a male intimate partner. "Table 33:
Ten-Year Arrest Trends," FBI: Uniform Crime Reporting, 2017, https://ucr
.fbi.gov/crime-in-the-u.s/2017/crime-in-the-u.s.-2017/topic-pages/tables
/table-33.

73   Community and societal factors: Claudia Garcia-Moreno, Alessandra Guedes, and Wendy Knerr, "Intimate Partner Violence," in *Understanding and Addressing Violence Against Women*, ed. Sarah Ramsay (Geneva: World Health Organization, 2012), http://apps.who.int/iris/bitstream/10665/77432/1/WHO_RHR_12.36_eng.pdf.

78   "The truth is that story": Jess McIntosh, "I Went on a Date with Eric Schneiderman. It Took Me Years to Process What Happened That Night," *Elle*, May 31, 2018, https://www.elle.com/culture/a20896599/eric-schneiderman-date-story-jess-mcintosh.

78   The United Nations Population Fund (UNFPA) estimated: Emma Batha and Ellen Wulfhorst, "Coronavirus to Have 'Catastrophic' Impact on Women with Domestic Abuse Up 20%," Reuters, April 28, 2020, https://www.reuters.com/article/us-health-coronavirus-women/coronavirus-to-have-catastrophic-impact-on-women-with-domestic-abuse-up-20-idUSKCN22A2BP.

79   I wrote an essay: Tanya Selvaratnam, "Where Can Domestic Violence Victims Turn During Covid-19?," *New York Times*, March 23, 2020, https://www.nytimes.com/2020/03/23/opinion/covid-domestic-violence.html.

79   Early in the global pandemic in China: Zhang Wanqing, "Domestic Violence Cases Surge During COVID-19 Epidemic," Sixth Tone, March 2, 2020, https://www.sixthtone.com/news/1005253/domestic-violence-cases-surge-during-covid-19-epidemic.

79   Spain reported: Amanda Taub, "A New Covid-19 Crisis: Domestic Abuse Rises Worldwide," *New York Times*, April 6, 2020, https://www.nytimes.com/2020/04/06/world/coronavirus-domestic-violence.html.

79   Canada announced: Omar Sachedina and Jonathan Forani, "Domestic Violence Increases with 'Stay Home' Pandemic Response," CTV News, April 6, 2020, https://www.ctvnews.ca/health/coronavirus/domestic-violence-increases-with-stay-home-pandemic-response-1.4885597.

80   Mexico took no steps: Maya Oppenheim, "Mexico Sees Almost 1,000 Women Murdered in Three Months as Domestic Abuse Concerns Rise amid Coronavirus," *Independent*, April 28, 2020, https://www.independent.co.uk/news/world/americas/mexico-coronavirus-domestic-violence-women-murder-femicide-lockdown-a9488321.html.

80   "I don't think": "Russia Seeks Protections for Domestic Abuse Victims During Coronavirus Lockdown," *Moscow Times*, April 22, 2020, https://www.themoscowtimes.com/2020/04/22/russia-seeks-protections-for-domestic-abuse-victims-during-coronavirus-lockdown-a70071.

80   Meanwhile, cities around the country: Madison Pauly and Julia Lurie, "Domestic Violence 911 Calls Are Increasing. Coronavirus Is Likely to Blame," *Mother Jones*, March 31, 2020, https://www.motherjones.com/crime-justice/2020/03/domestic-violence-abuse-coronavrius.

81   "the second-busiest month ever": Keith Collins and David Yaffe-Bellany, "About 2 Million Guns Were Sold in the U.S. as Virus Fears Spread," *New York Times*, April 1, 2020, https://www.nytimes.com/interactive/2020/04/01/business/coronavirus-gun-sales.html.

81   "We're never going to have": Diane von Furstenberg, "#InChargeAtHome with Gloria Steinem and Diane von Furstenberg," DVF, May 20, 2020, YouTube, https://www.youtube.com/watch?v=yIge8IBxNjo&feature=youtu.be, 39:47.

82   Intimate partner violence has been linked: "WHO: Addressing Violence Against Women: Key Achievements and Priorities," World Health Organization, 2018, http://apps.who.int/iris/bitstream/handle/10665/275982/WHO-RHR-18.18-eng.pdf?ua=1.

82   "The lifetime economic cost": "Preventing Intimate Partner Violence," 2.

82   "The United States spends": Rachel Louise Snyder, *No Visible Bruises: What We Don't Know About Domestic Violence Can Kill Us* (New York: Bloomsbury Publishing, 2019), 122.

82   a "rhetorical strategy": Kimberlé Crenshaw. "Mapping the Margins: Intersectionality, Identity Politics, and Violence Against Women of Color," *Stanford Law Review* 43, no. 6 (1991): 1241–99, https://sph.umd.edu/sites/default/files/files/Kimberle_Crenshaw_Mapping_the_Margins.pdf, 1259.

82   African Americans make up: Teresa Wiltz, "'A Pileup of Inequities': Why People of Color Are Hit Hardest by Homelessness," The Pew Charitable Trusts, March 29, 2019, https://www.pewtrusts.org/en/research-and-analysis/blogs/stateline/2019/03/29/a-pileup-of-inequities-why-people-of-color-are-hit-hardest-by-homelessness.

83   The majority of homeless women: Soraya Chemaly, *Rage Becomes Her: The Power of Women's Anger* (New York: Atria Books, 2019), 149.

83   African American and Hispanic women: Beryl Ann Cowan, "Incarcerated Women: Poverty, Trauma and Unmet Need," *The SES Indicator* 12, no. 1 (April 2019), https://www.apa.org/pi/ses/resources/indicator/2019/04/incarcerated-women.

83   The majority of incarcerated women: Karen L. Cox, "Most Women in Prison Are Victims of Domestic Violence. That's Nothing New," *Time*, October 2, 2017, https://time.com/4960309/domestic-violence-women-prison-history.

83   "wanted to leave her abusive husband": Ashley Southall, "Why a Drop in Domestic Violence Reports Might Not Be a Good Sign," *New York Times*, April 17, 2020, https://www.nytimes.com/2020/04/17/nyregion/new-york -city-domestic-violence-coronavirus.html.

83   "Women of color are often reluctant": Crenshaw, "Mapping the Margins," 1257.

83   According to a 2016 study: André B. Rosay, "Violence Against American Indian and Alaska Native Women and Men," *National Institute of Justice Journal*, June 1, 2016, https://nij.ojp.gov/topics/articles/violence-against-american -indian-and-alaska-native-women-and-men.

84   "One of our elders at home": Liz Hill, "New Film 'An Indigenous Response to MeToo'—Breaking the Silence for Healing," Censored News, April 4, 2018, https://bsnorrell.blogspot.com/2018/04/new-film-indigenous -response-to-metoo.html.

CHAPTER 10: THE PATTERN

106   "Certainly, Mr. Schneiderman": Danny Hakim and William K. Rash- baum, "New York's Attorney General in Battle with Trump," *New York Times*, December 26, 2017, https://www.nytimes.com/2017/12/26/nyregion/eric -schneiderman-attorney-general-new-york.html.

106   *GQ* ran a profile about Eric: Ben Schreckinger, "New York Attorney General Eric Schneiderman on What It Takes to Keep Trump in Check," *GQ*, November 29, 2017, https://www.gq.com/story/new-york-attorney-general-eric -schneiderman-trump-interview.

108   "More and more now": Sonali Deraniyagala, *Wave* (New York: Alfred A. Knopf, 2013), 226.

108   "To withhold words is power.": Terry Tempest Williams, *When Women Were Birds: Fifty-four Variations on Voice* (New York: Picador, 2012), 16.

CHAPTER 11: COMING FORWARD

116   "a man who could be": Andrew Prokop, "The Rob Porter Scandal Keeps Getting Worse for Trump's White House," Vox, February 9, 2018, https:// www.vox.com/policy-and-politics/2018/2/8/16988560/rob-porter-allegations -resigns.

116   Dahlia Lithwick wrote a piece: Dahlia Lithwick, "Rob Porter's History of Domestic Abuse Wasn't a Secret. It's Just That No One Cared," Slate, Febru- ary 8, 2018, https://slate.com/news-and-politics/2018/02/rob-porters-history -of-domestic-abuse-wasnt-a-secret.html.

116   "It typically took": Catharine A. MacKinnon, "#MeToo Has Done

What the Law Could Not," *New York Times*, February 4, 2018, https://www
.nytimes.com/2018/02/04/opinion/metoo-law-legal-system.html.

118 "he spoke at a lectern": Andrew Ross Sorkin, "Does a Lawsuit Now Help
the Weinstein Victims?," *New York Times*, February 12, 2018, https://www
.nytimes.com/2018/02/12/business/dealbook/weinstein-victims-lawsuit.html.

CHAPTER 12: THE ROLLER COASTER

129 "82% of respondents": Stephanie Zacharek, Eliana Dockterman, and
Haley Sweetland Edwards, "The Silence Breakers," *Time*, December 6, 2017,
http://time.com/time-person-of-the-year-2017-silence-breakers.

CHAPTER 13: THE FALLOUT

140 *"In the last several hours"*: Aaron Katersky, Josh Margolin, and Justin
Doom, "NY Attorney General Eric Schneiderman Resigns After Report He
Abused 4 Women," ABC News, May 8, 2018, https:// abcnews.go.com/Politics
/york-attorney-general-resign-reports-abuse-women/story?id=55002677.

140 *"I've known Eric"*: Jane Mayer and Ronan Farrow, "Four Women Accuse New York's Attorney General of Physical Abuse," *New Yorker*, May 7,
2018, https://www.newyorker.com/news/news-desk/four-women-accuse-new
-yorks-attorney-general-of-physical-abuse.

142 "One day in June 2018": Rebecca Traister, *Good and Mad: The Revolutionary Power of Women's Anger* (New York: Simon & Schuster, 2018), 219.

144 The Cut ran a feature: Madeleine Aggeler, "Eric Schneiderman and Men
Who Excuse Violence as 'Kink,'" The Cut, May 8, 2018, https://www.thecut
.com/2018/05/eric-schneiderman-sexual-assault-kink-bdsm.html.

144 ""Role play means two people": Alexa Tsoulis-Reay, "Here's How Consent and BDSM Role-Play Actually Work," The Cut, May 9, 2018, https://
www.thecut.com/2018/05/how-to-role-play-bdsm-for-beginners.html.

145 On the train, I read: Carolyn G. Heilbrun, *Writing a Woman's Life* (New
York: W. W. Norton and Company, 1988).

146 "told him that if Mr. Trump": Alan Feuer, "Lawyer for 2 Schneiderman
Accusers Brought Their Claims to Michael Cohen," *New York Times*, May 11, 2018,
https://www.nytimes.com/2018/05/11/nyregion/eric-schneiderman-michael
-cohen.html.

149 I'd made it onto *The Daily Show*: Trevor Noah, "Eric 'Champion of Women'
Schneiderman Falls to Me Too Movement," Comedy Central, May 8, 2018,
http://www.cc.com/video-clips/930keb/the-daily-show-with-trevor-noah
-eric—champion-of-women—schneiderman-falls-to-the-me-too-movement,
video, 5:22.

151   Later that summer, Samantha Bee spoke: Vulture Editors, "Samantha Bee and the *Full Frontal* Team Reflect on Their Wild Ride Since the Election," *Vulture*, August 24, 2018, http://www.vulture.com/2018/08/samantha-bee -full-frontal-vulture-fest.html.

155   That big story was about: Ronan Farrow, "As Leslie Moonves Negotiates His Exit from CBS, Six Women Raise New Assault and Harassment Claims," *New Yorker*, September 9, 2018, https://www.newyorker.com/news/news-desk /as-leslie-moonves-negotiates-his-exit-from-cbs-women-raise-new-assault -and-harassment-claims.

CHAPTER 14: THE LESSON

157   Forty-seven percent of white women: Molly Ball, "Donald Trump Didn't Really Win 52% of White Women in 2016," *Time*, October 18, 2018, https:// time.com/5422644/trump-white-women-2016.

158   "One year after Donald Trump": Rebecca Traister, *Good and Mad: The Revolutionary Power of Women's Anger* (New York: Simon & Schuster, 2018), 38.

158   "It's a Cromwell moment!": Quoted in David Remnick, "A Reckoning with Women Awaits Trump," *New Yorker*, February 11, 2018, https:// www.newyorker.com/news/daily-comment/a-reckoning-with-women-awaits -trump.

159   training programs for boys: Andrew Reiner, "Boy Talk: Breaking Masculine Stereotypes," *New York Times*, October 24, 2018, https://www.nytimes .com/2018/10/24/well/family/boy-talk-breaking-masculine-stereotypes.html.

159   "In every part of their lives": Brittney C. Cooper, *Eloquent Rage: A Black Feminist Discovers Her Superpower* (New York: Picador, 2018), 92.

160   "lost their jobs": Audrey Carlsen, Maya Salam, Claire Cain Miller, Denise Lu, Ash Ngu, Jugal K. Patel, and Zach Wichter, "#MeToo Brought Down 201 Powerful Men. Nearly Half of Their Replacements Are Women," *New York Times*, October 23, 2018, https://www.nytimes.com/interactive/2018/10/23 /us/metoo-replacements.html.

161   "The world's first mass movement": Catharine A. MacKinnon, "Where #MeToo Came From, and Where It's Going," *The Atlantic*, March 24, 2019, https://www.theatlantic.com/ideas/archive/2019/03/catharine-mackinnon -what-metoo-has-changed/585313.

161   "will have 'staying power'": Ariane de Vogue, "#MeToo Will Have Staying Power, Ruth Bader Ginsburg Insists," CNN, February 12, 2018, https:// www.cnn.com/2018/02/11/politics/ruth-bader-ginsburg-me-too-poppy -harlow/index.html.

161 "Everyone likes to remind me": Editors of The Cut, "Anita Hill Won, Even Though She Lost," The Cut, October 15, 2018, https://www.thecut .com/2018/10/women-and-power-chapter-one.html.

161 "If the Senate Judiciary Committee": Anita Hill, "Anita Hill: Let's Talk About How to End Sexual Violence," New York Times, May 9, 2019, https:// www.nytimes.com/2019/05/09/opinion/anita-hill-sexual-violence.html.

162 "Almost everybody was a jerk": Molly Langmuir, "What's Next for New Yorker Reporter Jane Mayer?," Elle, February 27, 2019, https://www.elle.com /culture/a26537529/jane-mayer-new-yorker-interview-kavanaugh.

162 "I am here today": Dylan Scott, "Read Christine Blasey Ford's Written Testimony: 'I Am Here Today Not Because I Want to Be. I Am Terrified,'" Vox, September 27, 2018, https://www.vox.com/2018/9/26/17907462/christine -blasey-ford-testimony-brett-kavanaugh-hearing.

163 "found that Republicans": Stephanie Zacharek, Eliana Dockterman, and Haley Sweetland Edwards, "The Silence Breakers," Time, December 6, 2017, http://time.com/time-person-of-the-year-2017-silence-breakers.

163 "called for a special working group": Joan Biskupic, "Federal Courts Say They'll Now Track Sexual Harassment Data," CNN, February 20, 2018, https://www.cnn.com/2018/02/20/politics/courts-sexual-harassment-data /index.html.

164 "There is no place in the Academy": Rory Carroll, "Hollywood After Weinstein: 'The Animals Have No Choice but to Be Civilized,'" The Guardian, January 1, 2018, https://www.theguardian.com/film/2018/jan/01/hollywood -sexual-misconduct-after-weinstein.

166 Jeffrey Epstein called himself: Julie K. Brown, "For Years, Jeffrey Epstein Abused Teen Girls, Police Say: A Timeline of His Case," Miami Herald, November 28, 2018, https://www.miamiherald.com/news/local/article221404845.html.

166 During the 2019 Sundance Film Festival: Trey Williams, "Former Weinstein Exec David Glasser Launches New Production Company 101 Studios," The Wrap, January 22, 2019, https://www.thewrap.com/former -weinstein-exec-david-glasser-launches-new-company-101-studios.

167 "It feels very odd to me": Mary McNamara, "Must Reads: Emma Thompson's Letter to Skydance: Why I Can't Work for John Lasseter," Los Angeles Times, February 26, 2019, https://www.latimes.com/entertainment /la-et-mn-emma-thompson-john-lasseter-skydance-20190226-story.html.

167 "Felony assault in New York State": Ginia Bellafante, "The #MeToo Movement Changed Everything. Can the Law Catch Up?," New York Times,

November 21, 2018, https://www.nytimes.com/2018/11/21/nyregion/metoo -movement-schneiderman-prosecution.html.

167   "Equal stature of men and women": de Vogue, "#MeToo Will Have Staying Power, Ruth Bader Ginsburg Insists."

167   "the only legal change": MacKinnon, "Where #MeToo Came From, and Where It's Going."

168   "remain physically non-violent": World Health Organization, "Violence by Intimate Partners," in *World Report on Violence and Health*, ed. Etienne G. Krug, Linda L. Dahlberg, James A. Mercy, Anthony B. Zwi, and Rafael Lozano (Geneva: World Health Organization, 2002), http://www.who.int /violence_injury_prevention/violence/global_campaign/en/chap4.pdf, 106.

168   His father said that Turner: Elle Hunt, "'20 Minutes of Action': Father Defends Stanford Student Son Convicted of Sexual Assault," *The Guardian*, June 5, 2016, https://www.theguardian.com/us-news/2016/jun/06/father -stanford-university-student-brock-turner-sexual-assault-statement.

169   "Men learn to regard rape": Soraya Chemaly, *Rage Becomes Her: The Power of Women's Anger* (New York: Atria Books, 2019), 126.

169   "[T]o girls everywhere": Katie J. M. Baker, "Here's the Powerful Letter the Stanford Victim Read to Her Attacker," BuzzFeed News, June 3, 2016, https://www.buzzfeednews.com/article/katiejmbaker/heres-the-powerful -letter-the-stanford-victim-read-to-her-ra.

169   Chanel Miller told her story: Chanel Miller, *Know My Name: A Memoir* (New York: Viking, 2019).

CHAPTER 15: MOVING FORWARD

172   "Ultimately, I take responsibility": Tanya Selvaratnam, "What Happened After I Shared My Story of Abuse by New York's Attorney General," *New York Times*, October 6, 2018, https://www.nytimes.com/2018/10/06/opinion /sunday/eric-schneiderman-abuse.html.

CODA (SIX MONTHS LATER)

178   "I believe the women": Alan Feuer, "Schneiderman Will Not Face Criminal Charges in Abuse Complaints," *New York Times*, November 8, 2018, https://www.nytimes.com/2018/11/08/nyregion/eric-schneiderman-abuse -charges.html.

178   "I recognize that": Ibid.

EPILOGUE

186 *She Said*: Jodi Kantor and Megan Twohey, *She Said: Breaking the Sexual Harassment Story That Helped Ignite a Movement* (New York: Penguin Press, 2019).

186 *Nobody's Victim*: Carrie Goldberg, *Nobody's Victim: Fighting Psychos, Stalkers, Pervs, and Trolls* (New York: Plume, 2019).

189 "The precise role of the artist": James Baldwin, "The Creative Process," in *Creative America* (New York: Ridge Press, 1962).

191 If the robin visits you: "Robin—Spirit Animal, Symbolism and Meaning," Dreaming and Sleeping, https://dreamingandsleeping.com/robin-spirit -animal-symbolism-and-meaning.

191 "What would happen": Terry Tempest Williams, *When Women Were Birds: Fifty-four Variations on Voice* (New York: Picador, 2012), 100.

BIBLIOGRAPHY

Aggeler, Madeleine. "Eric Schneiderman and Men Who Excuse Violence as 'Kink.'" The Cut, May 8, 2018. https://www.thecut.com/2018/05/eric -schneiderman-sexual-assault-kink-bdsm.html.

Alderman, Naomi. *The Power*. New York: Little, Brown and Company, 2016.

Atwood, Margaret. *The Handmaid's Tale*. New York: Anchor Books, 1986.

Baker, Katie J. M. "Here's the Powerful Letter the Stanford Victim Read to Her Attacker." BuzzFeed News, June 3, 2016. https://www.buzzfeednews .com/article/katiejmbaker/heres-the-powerful-letter-the-stanford-victim -read-to-her-ra.

Baldwin, James. "The Creative Process." In *Creative America*. New York: Ridge Press, 1962.

Ball, Molly. "Donald Trump Didn't Really Win 52% of White Women in 2016." *Time*, October 18, 2018. https://time.com/5422644/trump-white -women-2016.

Batha, Emma, and Ellen Wulfhorst. "Coronavirus to Have 'Catastrophic' Impact on Women with Domestic Abuse Up 20%." Reuters, April 28, 2020. https://www.reuters.com/article/us-health-coronavirus-women/coronavirus -to-have-catastrophic-impact-on-women-with-domestic-abuse-up-20-idUSK CN22A2BP.

Bellafante, Ginia. "The #MeToo Movement Changed Everything. Can the Law Catch Up?" *New York Times*, November 21, 2018. https://www.nytimes .com/2018/11/21/nyregion/metoo-movement-schneiderman-prosecution.html.

Biskupic, Joan. "Federal Courts Say They'll Now Track Sexual Harassment Data." CNN, February 20, 2018. https://www.cnn.com/2018/02/20/politics /courts-sexual-harassment-data/index.html.

Brown, Julie K. "For Years, Jeffrey Epstein Abused Teen Girls, Police Say: A Timeline of His Case." *Miami Herald*, November 28, 2018. https://www .miamiherald.com/news/local/article221404845.html.

Carlsen, Audrey, Maya Salam, Claire Cain Miller, Denise Lu, Ash Ngu, Jugal K. Patel, and Zach Wichter. "#MeToo Brought Down 201 Powerful Men. Nearly Half of Their Replacements Are Women." *New York Times*, October 23, 2018. https://www.nytimes.com/interactive/2018/10/23/us/metoo-replacements .html.

Carroll, Rory. "Hollywood After Weinstein: 'The Animals Have No Choice But to Be Civilized.'" *Guardian*, January 1, 2018. https://www.theguardian. com/film/2018/jan/01/hollywood-sexual-misconduct-after-weinstein.

Chemaly, Soraya. *Rage Becomes Her: The Power of Women's Anger*. New York: Atria Books, 2019.

Cohan, William D. "'Nothing About This Deal Feels Right to Me': Inside Harvey Weinstein's Other Nightmare." *Vanity Fair*, December 20, 2017. https://www.vanityfair.com/news/2017/12/harvey-weinstein-nightmare -finding-neverland-amfar-money.

Collins, Keith, and David Yaffe-Bellany. "About 2 Million Guns Were Sold in the U.S. as Virus Fears Spread." *New York Times*, April 1, 2020. https://www .nytimes.com/interactive/2020/04/01/business/coronavirus-gun-sales.html.

Cooper, Brittney C. *Eloquent Rage: A Black Feminist Discovers Her Superpower*. New York: Picador, 2018.

Cowan, Beryl Ann. "Incarcerated Women: Poverty, Trauma and Unmet Need." *The SES Indicator* 12, no. 1 (April 2019). https://www.apa.org/pi/ses/resources /indicator/2019/04/incarcerated-women.

Cox, Karen L. "Most Women in Prison Are Victims of Domestic Violence. That's Nothing New." *Time*, October 2, 2017. https://time.com/4960309 /domestic-violence-women-prison-history.

Crenshaw, Kimberlé. "Mapping the Margins: Intersectionality, Identity Politics, and Violence Against Women of Color." *Stanford Law Review* 43, no. 6 (1991): 1241–99. https://sph.umd.edu/sites/default/files/files/Kimberle_Crenshaw _Mapping_the_Margins.pdf.

de Becker, Gavin. *The Gift of Fear: And Other Survival Signals That Protect Us from Violence*. New York: Dell Publishing, 1997.

Deraniyagala, Sonali. *Wave*. New York: Alfred A. Knopf, 2013.

de Vogue, Ariane. "#MeToo Will Have Staying Power, Ruth Bader Ginsburg Insists." CNN, February 12, 2018. https://www.cnn.com/2018/02/11/politics /ruth-bader-ginsburg-me-too-poppy-harlow/index.html.

Editors of The Cut. "Anita Hill Won, Even Though She Lost." The Cut, October 15, 2018. https://www.thecut.com/2018/10/women-and-power-chapter -one.html.

Engel, Beverly. *The Emotionally Abusive Relationship: How to Stop Being Abused and How to Stop Abusing*. Hoboken, NJ: John Wiley and Sons, 2002.

Evans, Patricia. *The Verbally Abusive Relationship: How to Recognize It and How to Respond*. New York: Adams Media, 2010.

Farrow, Ronan. "As Leslie Moonves Negotiates His Exit from CBS, Six Women Raise New Assault and Harassment Claims." *New Yorker*, September 9, 2018. https://www.newyorker.com/news/news-desk/as-leslie-moonves-negotiates -his-exit-from-cbs-women-raise-new-assault-and-harassment-claims.

Feuer, Alan. "Lawyer for 2 Schneiderman Accusers Brought Their Claims to Michael Cohen." *New York Times*, May 11, 2018. https://www.nytimes .com/2018/05/11/nyregion/eric-schneiderman-michael-cohen.html.

———. "Schneiderman Will Not Face Criminal Charges in Abuse Complaints." *New York Times*, November 8, 2018. https://www.nytimes.com/2018 /11 /08 /nyregion/eric-schneiderman-abuse-charges.html.

Garcia-Moreno, Claudia, Alessandra Guedes, and Wendy Knerr. "Intimate Partner Violence," in *Understanding and Addressing Violence Against Women*, ed. Sarah Ramsay. Geneva: World Health Organization, 2012. http://apps.who .int/iris/bitstream/10665/77432/1/WHO_RHR_12.36_eng.pdf.

Goldberg, Carrie. *Nobody's Victim: Fighting Psychos, Stalkers, Pervs, and Trolls*. New York: Plume, 2019.

Grigoriadis, Vanessa. "'I Collect People, I Own People, I Can Damage People': The Curious Sociopathy of Jeffrey Epstein." *Vanity Fair*, August 26, 2019. https://www.vanityfair.com/news/2019/08/curious-sociopathy-of-jeffrey -epstein-ex-girlfriends.

Hakim, Danny, and William K. Rashbaum. "New York's Attorney General in Battle with Trump." *New York Times*, December 16, 2017. https://www.nytimes .com/2017/12/26/nyregion/eric-schneiderman-attorney-general-new-york.html.

Heilbrun, Carolyn G. *Writing a Woman's Life*. New York: W. W. Norton and Company, 1988.

Hill, Anita. "Anita Hill: Let's Talk About How to End Sexual Violence." *New York Times*, May 9, 2019. https://www.nytimes.com/2019/05/09/opinion/anita -hill-sexual-violence.html.

Hill, Liz. "New Film 'An Indigenous Response to #MeToo'—Breaking the Silence for Healing." Censored News, April 4, 2018. https://bsnorrell.blogspot .com/2018/04/new-film-indigenous-response-to-metoo.html.

Hunt, Elle. "'20 Minutes of Action': Father Defends Stanford Student Son Convicted of Sexual Assault." *Guardian*, June 5, 2016. https://www.theguardian .com/us-news/2016/jun/06/father-stanford-university-student-brock-turner -sexual-assault-statement.

Kantor, Jodi, and Megan Twohey. *She Said: Breaking the Sexual Harassment Story That Helped Ignite a Movement*. New York: Penguin Press, 2019.

Katersky, Aaron, Josh Margolin, and Justin Doom. "NY Attorney General Eric Schneiderman Resigns After Report He Abused 4 Women." ABC News, May 8, 2018. https://abcnews.go.com/Politics/york-attorney-general-resign -reports-abuse-women/story?id=55002677.

Langmuir, Molly. "What's Next for *New Yorker* Reporter Jane Mayer?" *Elle*, February 27, 2019. https://www.elle.com/culture/a26537529/jane-mayer-new -yorker-interview-kavanaugh.

Lithwick, Dahlia. "Rob Porter's History of Domestic Abuse Wasn't a Secret. It's Just That No One Cared." Slate, February 8, 2018. https://slate.com/news -and-politics/2018/02/rob-porters-history-of-domestic-abuse-wasnt-a-secret .html.

MacKinnon, Catharine A. "#MeToo Has Done What the Law Could Not." *New York Times*, February 4, 2018. https://www.nytimes.com/2018/02/04 /opinion/metoo-law-legal-system.html.

———. "Where #MeToo Came From, and Where It's Going." *Atlantic*, March 24, 2019. https://www.theatlantic.com/ideas/archive/2019/03/catharine -mackinnon-what-metoo-has-changed/585313.

Mayer, Jane, and Ronan Farrow. "Four Women Accuse New York's Attorney General of Physical Abuse." *New Yorker*, May 7, 2018. https://www.newyorker .com/news/news-desk/four-women-accuse-new-yorks-attorney-general-of -physical-abuse.

McArdle, Megan. "I Went Back to a Man Who Hit Me. I'm Still Thinking About Why." *Washington Post*, May 8, 2018. https://www.washingtonpost.com /opinions/i-went-back-to-the-man-who-hit-me-why/2018/05/08/0acb4c54 -52f2-11e8-abd8-265bd07a9859_story.html.

McIntosh, Jess. "I Went on a Date with Eric Schneiderman. It Took Me Years to Process What Happened That Night." *Elle*, May 31, 2018. https://www.elle com/culture/a20896599/eric-schneiderman-date-story-jess-mcintosh.

McNamara, Mary. "Must Reads: Emma Thompson's Letter to Skydance: Why I Can't Work for John Lasseter." *Los Angeles Times*, February 26, 2019. https:// www.latimes.com/entertainment/la-et-mn-emma-thompson-john-lasseter -skydance-20190226-story.html.

Meyer, Eileen Hoenigman. "How to Deal When a Colleague Is Threatened by You." Glassdoor, May 11, 2018. https://www.glassdoor.com/blog/threatened.

Meyerson, Harold. "The Man the Banks Fear Most." *The American Prospect*, April 23, 2012. https://prospect.org/power/man-banks-fear.

Miller, Chanel. *Know My Name: A Memoir*. New York: Viking, 2019.

Millon, Emma M., Han Yan M. Chang, and Tracey J. Shors. "Stressful Life Memories Relate to Ruminative Thoughts in Women with Sexual Violence History, Irrespective of PTSD." *Frontiers in Psychiatry*, September 5, 2018. https://www.frontiersin.org/articles/10.3389/fpsyt.2018.00311/full.

Morris, David J. *The Evil Hours: A Biography of Post-Traumatic Stress Disorder.* New York: Eamon Dolan Books, 2015.

"National Statistics." National Coalition Against Domestic Violence. https:// ncadv.org/statistics.

Noah, Trevor. "Eric 'Champion of Women' Schneiderman Falls to Me Too Movement." Comedy Central, May 8, 2018. http://www.cc.com/video-clips /930keb/the-daily-show-with-trevor-noah-eric—champion-of-women— schneiderman-falls-to-the-me-too-movement, 5:22.

Oppenheim, Maya. "Mexico Sees Almost 1,000 Women Murdered in Three Months as Domestic Abuse Concerns Rise amid Coronavirus." *Independent*, April 28, 2020. https://www.independent.co.uk/news/world/americas /mexico-coronavirus-domestic-violence-women-murder-femicide-lockdown -a9488321.html.

Pauly, Madison, and Julia Lurie. "Domestic Violence 911 Calls Are Increasing. Coronavirus Is Likely to Blame." *Mother Jones*, March 31, 2020. https:// www.motherjones.com/crime-justice/2020/03/domestic-violence-abuse -coronavrius.

"Preventing Intimate Partner Violence." Atlanta: Centers for Disease Control and Prevention, 2019. https://www.cdc.gov/violenceprevention/pdf/ipv -factsheet508.pdf.

Prokop, Andrew. "The Rob Porter Scandal Keeps Getting Worse for Trump's White House." Vox, February 9, 2018. https://www.vox.com/policy-and -politics/2018/2/8/16988560/rob-porter-allegations-resigns.

Ravitz, Jessica, and Arman Azad. "Memories That Last: What Sexual Assault Survivors Remember and Why." CNN, September 21, 2018. https://www.cnn .com/2018/09/21/health/memory-sexual-assault-ptsd/index.html.

Reiner, Andrew. "Boy Talk: Breaking Masculine Stereotypes." New York Times, October 24, 2018. https://www.nytimes.com/2018/10/24/well/family /boy-talk-breaking-masculine-stereotypes.html.

Remnick, David. "A Reckoning with Women Awaits Trump." New Yorker, February 11, 2018. https://www.newyorker.com/news/daily-comment/a-reckoning -with-women-awaits-trump.

Rosay, André B. "Violence Against American Indian and Alaska Native Women and Men." National Institute of Justice Journal, June 1, 2016. https://nij .ojp.gov/topics/articles/violence-against-american-indian-and-alaska-native -women-and-men.

"Russia Seeks Protections for Domestic Abuse Victims During Coronavirus Lockdown." Moscow Times, April 22, 2020. https://www.themoscowtimes .com/2020/04/22/russia-seeks-protections-for-domestic-abuse-victims-during -coronavirus-lockdown-a70071.

Sachedina, Omar, and Jonathan Forani. "Domestic Violence Increases with 'Stay Home' Pandemic Response." CTV News, April 6, 2020. https://www .ctvnews.ca/health/coronavirus/domestic-violence-increases-with-stay-home -pandemic-response-1.4885597.

Schneiderman, Eric. "Transforming the Liberal Checklist." The Nation, February 21, 2008. https://www.thenation.com/article/transforming-liberal-checklist.

Schreckinger, Ben. "New York Attorney General Eric Schneiderman on What It Takes to Keep Trump in Check." GQ, November 29, 2017. https:// www.gq.com/story/new-york-attorney-general-eric-schneiderman-trump -interview.

Scott, Dylan. "Read Christine Blasey Ford's Written Testimony: 'I Am Here Today Not Because I Want to Be. I Am Terrified.'" Vox, September 27, 2018. https://www.vox.com/2018/9/26/17907462/christine-blasey-ford-testimony -brett-kavanaugh-hearing.

Selvaratnam, Tanya. "What Happened After I Shared My Story of Abuse by New York's Attorney General." New York Times, October 6, 2018. https://www .nytimes.com/2018/10/06/opinion/sunday/eric-schneiderman-abuse.html.

———. "Where Can Domestic Violence Victims Turn During Covid-19?" *New York Times*, March 23, 2020. https://www.nytimes.com/2020/03/23 /opinion/covid-domestic-violence.html.

Snyder, Rachel Louise. *No Visible Bruises: What We Don't Know About Domestic Violence Can Kill Us.* New York: Bloomsbury Publishing, 2019.

Sorkin, Andrew Ross. "Does a Lawsuit Now Help the Weinstein Victims?" *New York Times*, February 12, 2018. https://www.nytimes.com/2018/02/12 /business/dealbook/weinstein-victims-lawsuit.html.

Southall, Ashley. "Why a Drop in Domestic Violence Reports Might Not Be a Good Sign." *New York Times*, April 17, 2020. https://www.nytimes .com/2020/04/17/nyregion/new-york-city-domestic-violence-coronavirus .html.

Stark, Evan. *Coercive Control: How Men Entrap Women in Personal Life.* New York: Oxford University Press, 2007.

"Table 33: Ten-Year Arrest Trends." FBI: Uniform Crime Reporting, 2017. https://ucr.fbi.gov/crime-in-the-u.s/2017/crime-in-the-u.s.-2017/topic-pages /tables/table-33.

Taub, Amanda. "A New Covid-19 Crisis: Domestic Abuse Rises Worldwide." *New York Times*, April 6, 2020. https://www.nytimes.com/2020/04/06/world /coronavirus-domestic-violence.html.

Traister, Rebecca. *Good and Mad: The Revolutionary Power of Women's Anger.* New York: Simon & Schuster, 2018.

Tsoulis-Reay, Alexa. "Here's How Consent and BDSM Role-Play Actually Work." The Cut, May 9, 2018. https://www.thecut.com/2018/05/how-to-role -play-bdsm-for-beginners.html.

Twohey, Megan. "Tumult After AIDS Fund-Raiser Supports Harvey Weinstein Production." *New York Times*, September 23, 2017. https://www.nytimes.com /2017/09/23/nyregion/harvey-weinstein-charity.html.

von Furstenberg, Diane. "#InChargeAtHome with Gloria Steinem and Diane von Furstenberg." DVF, May 20, 2020. YouTube. https://www.youtube.com /watch?v=yIge8IBxNjo&feature=youtu.be, 39:47.

Vulture Editors. "Samantha Bee and the *Full Frontal* Team Reflect on Their Wild Ride Since the Election." Vulture, August 24, 2018. http://www.vulture .com/2018/08/samantha-bee-full-frontal-vulture-fest.html.

Wang, Amy B. "'Complicit' Is the 2017 Word of the Year, According to Dictionary.com." *Washington Post*, November 27, 2017. https://www.washingtonpost

.com/news/the-intersect/wp/2017/11/27/complicit-is-the-2017-word-of-the
-year-according-to-dictionary-com.

"WHO: Addressing Violence Against Women: Key Achievements and Priorities."
World Health Organization, 2018. http://apps.who.int/iris/bitstream/handle
/10665/275982/WHO-RHR-18.18-eng.pdf?ua=1.

Williams, Terry Tempest. *When Women Were Birds: Fifty-four Variations on
Voice.* New York: Picador, 2012.

Williams, Trey. "Former Weinstein Exec David Glasser Launches New Production Company 101 Studios." The Wrap, January 22, 2019. https://www
.thewrap.com/former-weinstein-exec-david-glasser-launches-new-company
-101-studios.

Wiltz, Teresa. "'A Pileup of Inequities': Why People of Color Are Hit Hardest
by Homelessness." The Pew Charitable Trusts, March 29, 2019. https://www
.pewtrusts.org/en/research-and-analysis/blogs/stateline/2019/03/29/a-pileup
-of-inequities-why-people-of-color-are-hit-hardest-by-homelessness.

World Health Organization. "Violence by Intimate Partners," in *World Report
on Violence and Health*, eds. Etienne G. Krug, Linda L. Dahlberg, James A.
Mercy, Anthony B. Zwi, and Rafael Lozano. Geneva: World Health Organization, 2002. http://www.who.int/violence_injury_prevention/violence/global
_campaign/en/chap4.pdf.

Zacharek, Stephanie, Eliana Dockterman, and Haley Sweetland Edwards.
"The Silence Breakers." *Time*, December 6, 2017. http://time.com/time-person
-of-the-year-2017-silence-breakers.

Zhang, Wanqing. "Domestic Violence Cases Surge During COVID-19
Epidemic." Sixth Tone, March 2, 2020. https://www.sixthtone.com/news
/1005253/domestic-violence-cases-surge-during-covid-19-epidemic.

ABOUT THE AUTHOR

TANYA SELVARATNAM is the author of *The Big Lie: Motherhood, Feminism, and the Reality of the Biological Clock*. Her essays have been published in the *New York Times*, *Vogue*, *The Art Newspaper*, SheKnows, *Glamour*, McSweeney's Internet Tendency, and on CNN, and she has been a fellow at Yaddo and Blue Mountain Center. She is an Emmy-nominated and Webby-winning film-maker, and she has been a producer for Aubin Pictures, For Freedoms, Glamour Women of the Year, the Meteor, Planned Parenthood, and the Vision & Justice Project.